Debbie Mumm celebrates **20** years of Creativity 1986~2006

Memories &
Milestones

By Debbie Mumm®

Created for Leisure Arts by Debbie Mumm®

CONTENTS

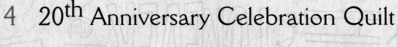

Dear Friends,

It's hard to believe that twenty years have already gone by! When I began my business in 1986, I never dreamed that it would evolve and grow the way it has. I really started my company as an opportunity to express my own creativity. I also wanted to share that with other people who have the same passions. This milestone anniversary brings memories of both happy and bittersweet moments, achievements and challenges and, most importantly, many wonderful friendships and working relationships.

This milestone for my company caused me to think of all the different milestones that are significant events and markers throughout a lifetime. What better way to celebrate a milestone than with a handmade, keepsake quilt. So we've developed more than twenty quilts and accessory projects, hoping each will become as meaningful a treasure as the milestone it commemorates.

From the arrival of a new baby to a creative childhood; from college-bound to the joyous union; celebrating friendship or saying thank-you; providing comfort in a time of crisis or embarking upon retirement, we've presented a quilt for every meaningful life passage.

Memorable occasions at the Mumm Studio are often celebrated with a group quilt, so for this book, I invited colleagues and friends that have been important to my business to make a block for my 20th Anniversary Quilt. You'll find ideas for your own group quilt within these pages.

So take a little time to reflect on the many defining moments of your life and envision those yet to come as you thumb through this book. Look for my own memories and milestones from the last twenty years sprinkled throughout the pages as well.

And, please accept my gratitude to you for participating in twenty years of quilts, comfort, and friendship.

With love and appreciation to all my friends,

 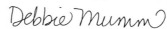

A Meaningful Milestone...

...is often shared by many. In a business like mine, **teams** of artists and designers, writers and editors, licensing partners and business colleagues have all played **an important part** in the success and growth of my company.

In a family, **each person contributes** to the joy, the nurturing, and the memories of the entire **family**.

Among **friends**, joys and sorrows, hardships and happy occasions, laughs and confidential conversations are **shared** creating an everlasting bond.

What better way to **celebrate a milestone** occasion than with a group quilt? Each person contributes a special block to make a keepsake quilt to be **treasured forever** by the lucky recipient.

20th Anniversary Celebration Quilt

At the Debbie Mumm Studio, we often celebrate special occasions with the gift of a group quilt. Over the years, we have made dozens of baby and wedding quilts and a variety of memory quilts. A group quilt is a fun way to mark a special event with a lasting keepsake. So, in keeping with the Mumm Studio tradition, we asked twenty quilters who have been important to the development of the company to join us in making a keepsake quilt to mark this important anniversary for me and my company.

To give you some ideas for making your own group quilts, we've created a list of fundamentals that we've found work well in planning a group quilt. Also included are brief instructions and appliqué patterns for the appliqué blocks in this quilt. Please refer to page 93 for general appliqué instructions. Fabric requirements and detailed directions for the pieced blocks are listed by block.

Fundamentals for a Group Quilt

1. Choose a color scheme and theme for the quilt based on the recipient's preferences.

2. Select 3-5 fabrics to give the quilt a cohesive color scheme. For the Anniversary Quilt, we chose six—one tan, two reds and three greens. A light, a medium, and a dark should be included in your fabric selections.

3. Decide on a block size. We chose 9" finished blocks which generally is an easy measurement to work with for pieced blocks.

4. Provide each person in the group with written instructions to include the occasion, theme of the quilt, any general guidelines, size of the block (specify 9½" unfinished, blocks will be 9" when sewn into the quilt), and due date.

5. Provide each participant with squares of each of the chosen fabrics cut at least ½" larger than the finished block size (in our case 10"). Ask that they use at least two or three of the fabrics provided in their blocks. Other fabrics from their stashes can also be used.

6. It's a good idea to request two or three more blocks than needed in case someone cannot meet the timeline. If more blocks are received than are needed, place on back of quilt with a special message or turn blocks into pillows.

7. When blocks have been collected, set a date for volunteers to get together to arrange and sew the blocks together.

8. On the sewing day, arrange the blocks on a flannel wall, if available, or the floor. Balance colors, motifs, and styles when arranging. Decide if sashing is needed or desired. Select borders.

9. Use masking tape to number the blocks so you can keep them in order. Use an assembly line to sew blocks together. Station some volunteers at ironing boards to make the process quicker. When the quilt top is complete, have a volunteer do the quilting or take up a collection for professional long-arm quilting. Ask a volunteer to bind the quilt. Don't forget to add a label including the date and the occasion. Present the quilt to the recipient at a group meeting.

HEN AND CHICKS BLOCK (Block One) ~ Contributor: Nancy Kirkland

A prodigious and accomplished quilter, Nancy's name appears in almost all of Debbie's quilting books—first as a hand quilter, then as principal seamstress for the last five years. Even with all that sewing, Nancy still finds time to use left-over bits and pieces to make quilts for charity. An avid bicyclist, skier, and swimmer, Nancy is also a new grandmother.

Instructions for the classic Hen and Chicks begin on page 8.

PLAYFUL PANSIES BLOCK (Block Two) ~ Contributor: Georgie Gerl

A lifetime of creativity has enabled Georgie to juggle her work in the family business as a designer and stained glass glazier and her work with Debbie as a quilt and craft designer. In between those occupations, Georgie enjoys four children now grown, spends time with her husband, Tim, and serves as an officer with the local quilt guild. Georgie's work can also be seen in Asian Fabric Magazine by Kona Bay Fabrics.

The pansy pattern is based on Debbie's artwork and is on page 17. Stems, vines, and flower centers were hand-embroidered and a black bead accents the flower centers. Crazy Quilt-style borders surround center motif, finished with a narrow straight border.

FRIENDSHIP AT SEA BLOCK (Block Three) ~ Contributor: Pat Tobin

Pat has the ideal job—she combines quilting with cruising! The organizer of numerous quilting cruises, Pat has worked with Debbie on two Debbie Mumm cruises—the Creative Woman Cruise in 2005 and the 20th Anniversary Cruise in 2006. Pat and her husband, Len, are devoted to raising money for cancer research and enjoy their children and grandchildren. Their household is ruled by two spoiled dogs.

Instructions for Friendship at Sea begin on page 9.

ANGELS ALL AROUND BLOCK (Block Four) ~ Contributor: Kathy Rickel

A novice quilter, Kathy learned to quilt after going to work at the Debbie Mumm Studio as art and graphics assistant. Mother of a toddler, Kat is working on completing several of her grandmother's quilt tops during naptime quilt sessions. This native Alaskan also enjoys working on the family's 100-year-old farmhouse, beading, camping, and visiting their large extended family with husband, Dal.

Angel pattern is adapted from Debbie's Angel of the Morning artwork and is on page 16. Kat used lightweight fusible web to adhere the appliqués and hand embroidery with a blanket stitch to finish. A yo-yo and three beads decorate the center and a border was added to finish the block.

STARS FROM THE STACKS BLOCK (Block Five) ~ Contributor: Pamela Mostek

A high school art teacher and compulsive hobby quilter, Pam made the move from hobbyist to professional by going to work for Debbie, first as a creative and editorial assistant and later as managing editor. Pam began her own design company in 2000, Making Lemonade Designs, which publishes her patterns and books. She is also the author of five books published by Martingale & Company and designs fabric for the quilting industry.

Stars from the Stacks uses a rail fence technique for the background. The raw-edge appliqué shapes are an enlargement of the star flowers in one of the principal fabrics.

CHECKERBOARD STAR BLOCK (Block Six) ~ Contributor: Susan Nelsen

"My first thought for designing a block for Debbie was 'Checkerboard', says Susan. While working for Debbie as a quilt designer, Susan had many opportunities to design quilts incorporating Debbie's favorite motif. When Susan left Spokane, she started her own quilt pattern company, Rasmatazz Designs and has published one book and numerous patterns.

Instructions for Checkerboard Star begin on page 10.

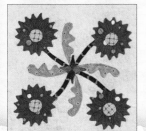

MUMM FLOWER BLOCK (Block Seven) ~ Contributor: Nancy Kirkland

A quilting over-achiever, Nancy has participated in many of the Mumm group quilts and knew that one of the challenges is a good balance of appliqué blocks to pieced blocks. Nancy did one of each type so we could select whichever we needed. Of course, we liked them both so well that both found a place in this quilt.

Applique patterns for the Mumm Flower Block are on page 16. To hand appliqué as Nancy did, add ¼" to all sides. For quick-fuse appliqué, use lightweight fusible web and finish edges as desired.

Continued on Page 18

20th Anniversary Celebration Quilt

20th Anniversary Celebration Quilt 58½" x 69½"	FIRST CUT		SECOND CUT	
	Number of Strips or Pieces	Dimensions	Number of Pieces	Dimensions
FABRICS FOR ALL BLOCKS				
Tan 1½ yards (1½ yards)				
Red 1½ yards (⅝ yard)				
Dark Red 1½ yards (⅝ yard)				
Light Green 1½ yards (⅝ yard)				
Medium Green 1½ yards (⅜ yard)				
Dark Green 1½ yards (⅞ yard)				
Sashing 1⅙ yards	14	2½" x 42"	15	2½" x 9½"
BORDERS				
First Border ¼ yard	6	1" x 42"		
Second Border ⅓ yard	6	1¼" x 42"		
Outside Border 2 yards OR 1 yard	2 2 6	69" x 5" (cut lengthwise) 49" x 5" (cut lengthwise) 5" x 42"		
Binding ⅝ yard	7	2¾" x 42"		

> Yardage is based on a 10" square for each of twenty participants - actual amounts used are noted in red

Backing - 3⅔ yards
Batting - 66" x 77"
Lightweight Fusible Web - 1½ yards
Heavyweight Fusible Web - ¼ yard
Appliqués - Assorted Scraps
Embellishments - Small buttons, beads, embroidery floss

Getting Started

Fabric requirements and cutting instructions for each pieced block are listed with the block. Read block construction instructions before beginning and use ¼"-wide seam allowance throughout. Blocks measure 9½" square unfinished. Most blocks use Quick Corner Triangles in construction. Refer to Quick Corner Triangles on page 92. Refer to Accurate Seam Allowance on page 92. Whenever possible, use the Assembly Line Method on page 92.

Block One~Hen and Chicks

Fabrics for Block One

Tan - Eight 2" x 3½" pieces
    Twenty 2" squares
Dark Red - Twelve 2" squares
Lt Green - Two 3½" squares
Med Green - Four 2" x 3½" pieces
Dark Green - Two 3½" squares

Making Block One

1. Refer to Quick Corner Triangles on page 92. Making a quick corner triangle, sew one 2" tan square to one 2" dark red square as shown. Press. Make eight.

Tan = 2 x 2
Dark Red = 2 x 2
Make 8

2. Sew together one unit from step 1 and one 2" tan square. Press. Sew this unit to one 2" x 3½" tan piece. Press. Make four.

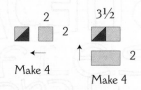

Make 4
Make 4

3. Making a quick corner triangle unit, sew one unit from step 2 to one 3½" dark green square, noting direction of drawn line to seams as shown. Prior to stitching, flip back unit to make sure positioning is correct. Press. Make four, two of each combination using light green and dark green squares as shown.

Unit from step 2
Dark Green = 3½ x 3½
Light Green = 3½ x 3½
Make 4
(2 of each combination)

4. Sew units from step 3 together in pairs as shown. Press. Make two. Sew units together as shown. Press, twisting intersection at center. (See page 67, Twisting Seams.)

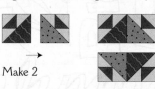

Make 2

Twist seams

5. Making quick corner triangle units, sew two 2" tan squares to one 2" x 3½" medium green piece as shown. Press. Make four.

Tan = 2 x 2
Medium Green = 2 x 3½
Make 4

6. Sew one unit from step 5 between two units from step 1 as shown. Press. Make two.

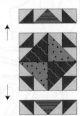

Make 2

7. Sew unit from step 4 between two units from step 6 as shown. Press.

8. Making a quick corner triangle unit, sew one 2" dark red square to one 2" x 3½" tan piece as shown. Press. Make four, two of each variation.

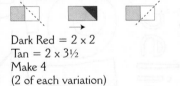

Dark Red = 2 x 2
Tan = 2 x 3½
Make 4
(2 of each variation)

9. Sew one unit from step 5 between two units from step 8 as shown. Press. Make two.

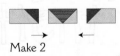

Make 2

10. Sew unit from step 7 between two units from step 9 as shown. Press. Block One measures 9½" square.

Block One measures 9½" square

Block Three~ Friendship at Sea

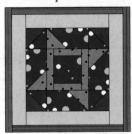

Fabrics for Block Three
Tan - Two 1½" x 8½" pieces
    Two 1½" x 6½" pieces
Red - One 2½" square
    Four 2" x 3½" pieces
    Four 2" squares
Dark Red - Four 2" squares
Light Green - Four 2" squares
    Two 1" x 3½" pieces
    Two 1" x 2½" pieces
Med. Green - Two 1" x 9½" pieces
    Two 1" x 8½" pieces

Making Block Three

1. Sew 2½" red square between two 1" x 2½" light green pieces as shown. Press. Sew unit between two 1" x 3½" light green pieces as shown. Press.

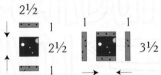

2. Refer to Quick Corner Triangles on page 92. Making a quick corner triangle, sew one 2" light green square to one 2" x 3½" red piece as shown. Press. Make four.

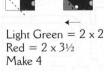

Light Green = 2 x 2
Red = 2 x 3½
Make 4

3. Sew unit from step 1 between two units from step 2 as shown. Press.

4. Making a quick corner triangle unit, sew one 2" red square to one 2" dark red square as shown. Press. Make four.

Dark Red = 2 x 2
Red = 2 x 2
Make 4

5. Sew one unit from step 2 between two units from step 4 as shown. Press. Make two.

Make 2

6. Sew unit from step 3 between two units from step 5 as shown. Press.

7. Sew unit from step 6 between two 1½" x 6½" tan pieces. Press seams toward border. Sew unit between two 1½" x 8½" tan pieces as shown. Press.

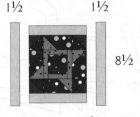

8. Sew unit from step 7 between two 1" x 8½" medium green pieces. Press seams toward border. Sew unit between two 1" x 9½" medium green pieces as shown. Press. Block Three measures 9½" square.

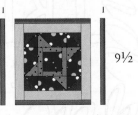

Block Three measures 9½" square

Block Six~ Checkerboard Star

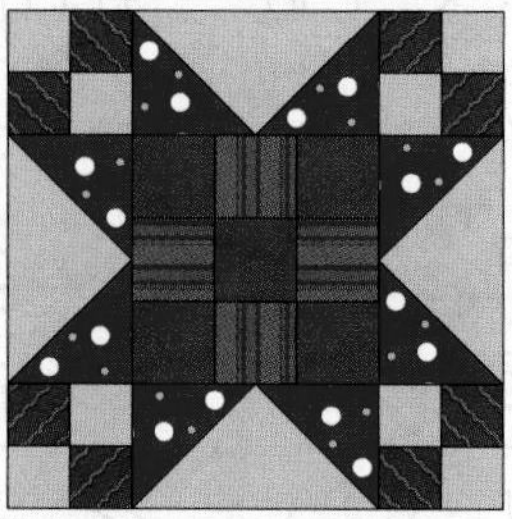

Fabrics for Block Six

Tan - Four 2¾" x 5" pieces
Eight 1 ⅝ " squares
Red - Eight 2¾" squares
Dark Red - Five 2" squares
Med. Green - Four 2" squares
Dark Green - Eight 1 ⅝ " squares

Making Block Six

1. Sew one 1⅝" dark green square to one 1⅝" tan square. Make eight. Sew together in pairs as shown. Press. Make four

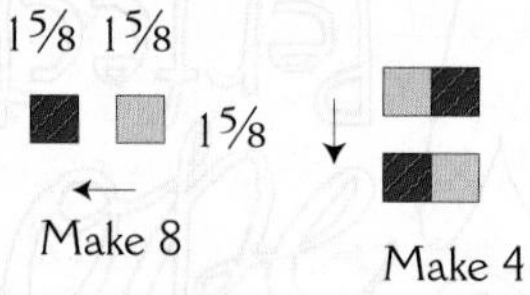
1⅝ 1⅝
1⅝
Make 8
Make 4

2. Refer to Quick Corner Triangles on page 92. Making quick corner triangle units, sew two 2¾" red squares to one 2¾" x 5" tan piece as shown. Press. Make four.

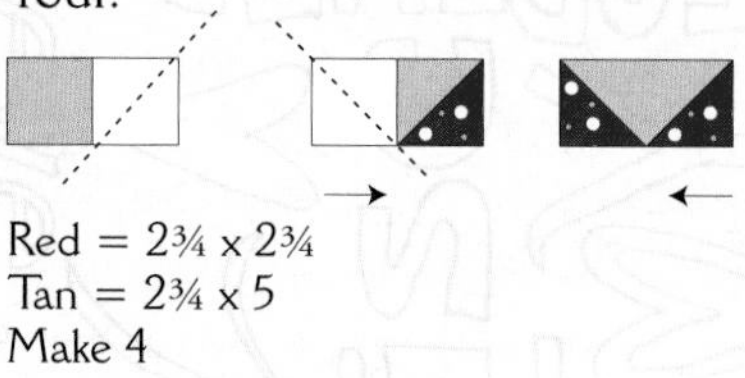
Red = 2¾ x 2¾
Tan = 2¾ x 5
Make 4

3. Sew one unit from step 2 between two units from step 1. Press. Make two.

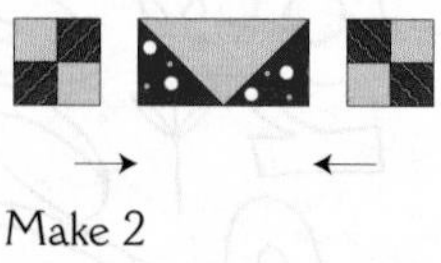
Make 2

4. Sew one 2" light green square between two 2" dark red squares as shown. Press. Make two. Sew one 2" dark red square between two 2" medium green squares as shown. Press.

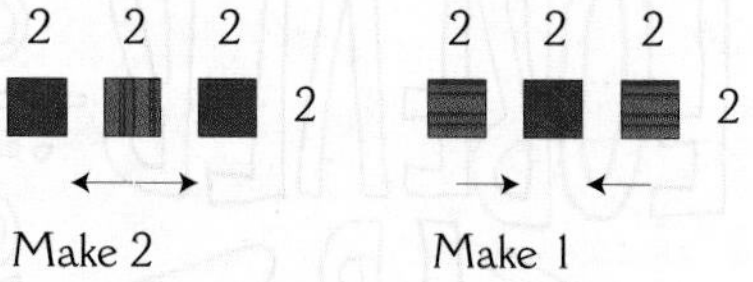
2 2 2
2
Make 2
2 2 2
2
Make 1

5. Sew units from step 4 together as shown. Press.

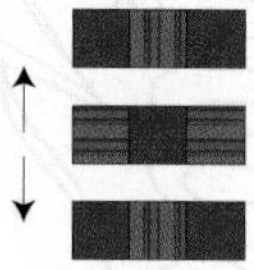

6. Sew unit from step 5 between two units from step 2 as shown. Press. Sew unit between two units from step 3 as shown. Press. Block Six measures 9½" square.

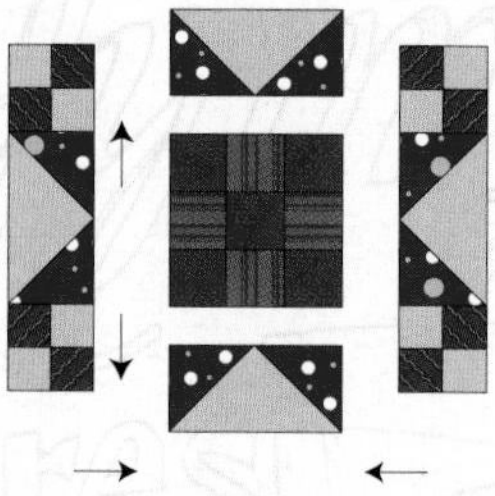

Block Six measures 9½" square

Block Eight~ Cat's Cradle

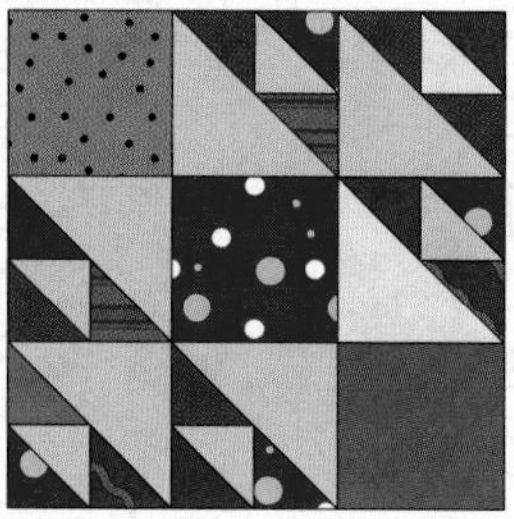

Fabrics for Block Eight

Tan - Six 3½" squares
Six 2" squares
Assorted Reds - One 3½" square
Three 2" x 3½" pieces
Seven 2" squares
Assorted Greens -
Two 3½" squares
Three 2" x 3½" pieces
Five 2" squares

Making Block Eight

Since this block contains assorted tans, reds, and greens, no distinction is used in the cutting chart. Refer to photo on page 8 and block layout and diagrams if a variety of shades is desired.

1. Refer to Quick Corner Triangles on page 92. Making a quick corner triangle unit, sew one 2" tan square to one 2" red square as shown. Press. Make four. Making quick corner triangle units, sew one 2" tan square to one 2" green square as shown. Press. Make two.

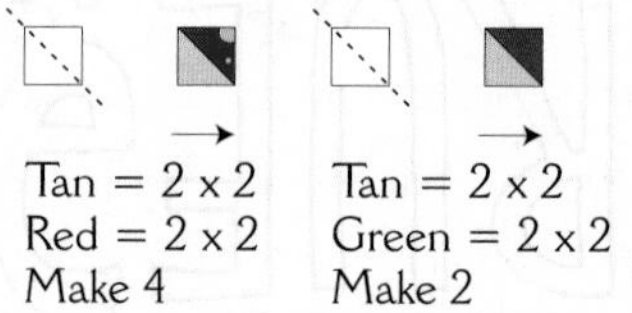
Tan = 2 x 2
Red = 2 x 2
Make 4
Tan = 2 x 2
Green = 2 x 2
Make 2

2. Referring to diagrams, sew units from step 1 to 2" green or red squares as shown. Press. Make six in assorted combinations as shown.

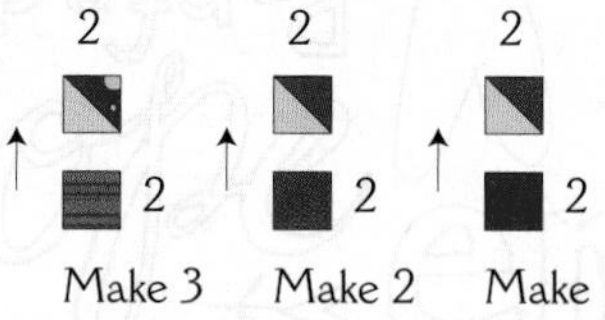
2
2
Make 3
2
2
Make 2
2
2
Make 1

3. Sew units from step 2 to 2" x 3½" red or green pieces as shown. Press. Make six in four combinations as shown.

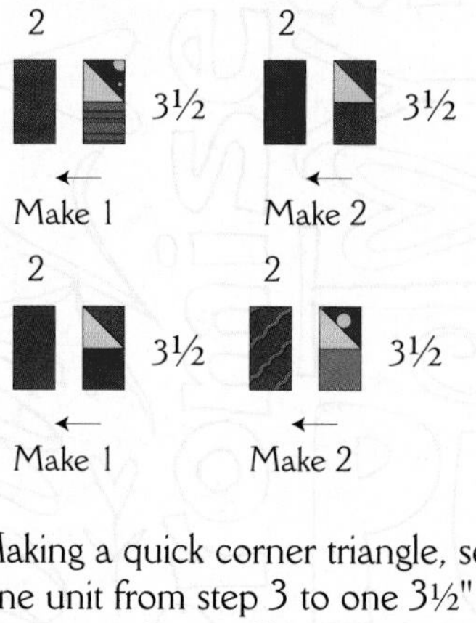
2
3½
Make 1
2
3½
Make 2
2
3½
Make 1
2
3½
Make 2

4. Making a quick corner triangle, sew one unit from step 3 to one 3½" tan square as shown. Prior to sewing, flip back unit to make sure positioning is correct. Press. Make six.

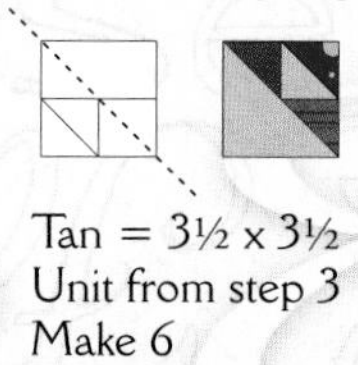
Tan = 3½ x 3½
Unit from step 3
Make 6

5. Referring to diagram, arrange two 3½" green squares, one 3½" red square, and units from step 4. Sew units together as shown. Press. Block eight measures 9½" square.

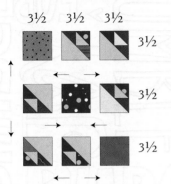

Block Eight measures 9½" square

Block Nine~ Sewing Circle

Fabrics for Block Nine

Tan - One 5" square
    Four 2¾" x 5" pieces
    Four 2¾" squares
Red - Two 2¾" squares
    Two 1⅝" squares
Dark Red - Two 2¾" squares
    Two 1⅝" squares
Lt Green - Two 2¾" squares
    Two 1⅝" squares
Dark Green - Two 2¾" squares
    Two 1⅝" squares

Making Block Nine

1. Refer to Quick Corner Triangles on page 92. Making quick corner triangle units, sew 1⅝" squares in assorted colors to four 2¾" tan squares as shown. Press. Make four, one of each color combination.

Red or Green = 1⅝ x 1⅝
Tan = 2¾ x 2¾
Make 4
(1 of each color combination)

2. Making quick corner triangle units, sew one 2¾" dark red square and one 2¾" light green square to one 2¾" x 5" tan piece as shown. Press. Referring to diagram, make four, one of each combination.

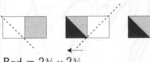

Red = 2¾ x 2¾
Green = 2¾ x 2¾
Tan = 2¾ x 5

Make 4
(1 of each combination)

3. Sew one unit from step 2 between two units from step 1 as shown. Press. Make two.

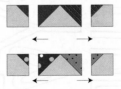

Make 2
(1 of each combination)

4. Making quick corner triangle units, sew four 1⅝" squares in assorted colors to one 5" tan square as shown. Press.

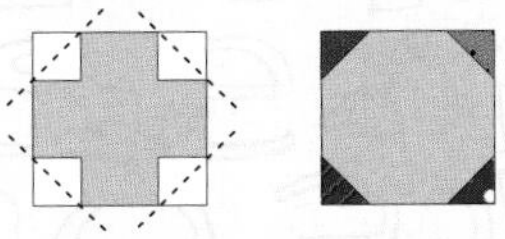

Reds and Greens = 1⅝ x 1⅝
Tan = 5 x 5

5. Sew unit from step 4 between two units from step 2 as shown. Press. Sew this unit between two units from step 3 as shown. Press. Block Nine measures 9½" square.

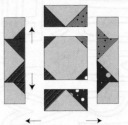

Block Nine measures 9½" square

Block Eleven~ Crossed Paths

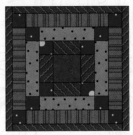

Fabrics for Block Eleven

Red - Twelve 1½" squares
Dark Red - One 2½" square
Light Green - Four 1½" x 4½" pieces
Med. Green - Four 1½" x 6½" pieces
Dark Green - Two 1" x 9½" pieces
    Two 1" x 8½" pieces
    Four 1½" x 2½" pieces

Making Block Eleven

1. Sew one 1½" x 2½" dark green piece between two 1½" red squares as shown. Press. Make two.

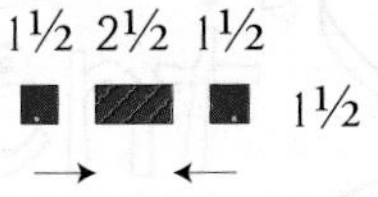

1½ 2½ 1½

 1½

Make 2

2. Sew one 2½" dark red square between two 1½" x 2½" dark green pieces as shown. Press. Sew unit between two units from step 1 as shown. Press.

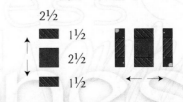

3. Sew one 1½" x 4½" light green piece between two 1½" red squares as shown. Press. Make two.

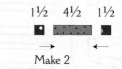

Make 2

4. Sew unit from step 2 between two 1½" x 4½" light green pieces as shown. Press. Sew unit between two units from step 3 as shown. Press.

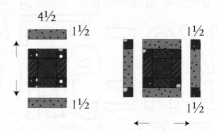

5. Sew one 1½" x 6½" med. green piece between two 1½" red squares as shown. Press. Make two.

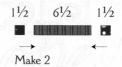

Make 2

6. Sew unit from step 4 between two 1½" x 6½" med green pieces as shown. Press. Sew unit between two units from step 5 as shown. Press.

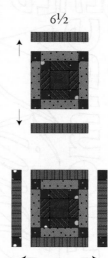

7. Sew unit from step 6 between two 1" x 8½" dark green pieces as shown. Press. Sew unit between two 1" x 9½" dark green pieces as shown. Press. Block Eleven measures 9½" square.

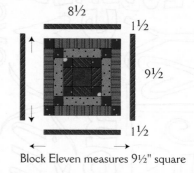

Block Eleven measures 9½" square

Block Twelve~ Butterfly Whirl

Fabrics for Block Twelve

Tan - Sixteen 2¾" squares

Assorted Reds - Eight 2¾" squares
One 1¾" circle

Assorted Greens - Four 2¾" squares

Black - Four 1½" x 4½" pieces

Appliqués - Assorted scraps

Heavyweight Fusible Web - ⅛ yard

Making Block Twelve

1. Refer to Making Quick Corner Triangles on page 92. Making a quick corner triangle, sew one 2¾" tan fabric square to one 2¾" red fabric square. Press. Make twelve, eight red and tan and four green and tan.

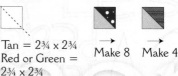

Tan = 2¾ x 2¾
Red or Green = 2¾ x 2¾   Make 8   Make 4

2. Arrange and sew two 2¾" tan fabric squares, and two units, one of each color, from step 1 as shown. Press. Make two.

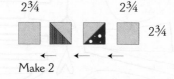

Make 2

3. Arrange and sew four units, one green and three red, from step 1 as shown. Press. Make two.

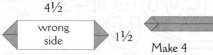

Make 2

4. Sew rows from steps 2 and 3 together as shown. Press. Block measures 9½" square.

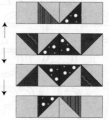

Block Twelve measures 9½" square

Adding the Appliqués

1. Place one 1½" x 4½" black fabric piece right side down, fold corners as shown, and press. Fold both long edges of fabric to center and press.

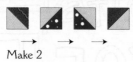

wrong side   1½   Make 4

2. Using ⅛"-long stitches, baste fabric as shown. Gently pull thread to gather stitches to make butterfly body 1¾" long. Tie thread to anchor. Make four.

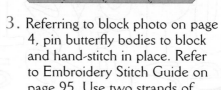

3. Referring to block photo on page 4, pin butterfly bodies to block and hand-stitch in place. Refer to Embroidery Stitch Guide on page 95. Use two strands of embroidery floss and a stem stitch to sew antennae, ending with a French knot.

4. Refer to Quick-Fuse Appliqué on page 93. Use patterns on page 17 to trace four light petals, four dark petals, and four leaves on fusible web. Use assorted scraps to prepare flower pieces for fusing. Cut out flower pieces and fuse to wrong side of matching fabrics. Cut pieces just inside leaf and petal shapes. Referring to block photo, arrange and tack flower pieces in center of block.

5. Use 1¾" red fabric circle to make a yo-yo and sew to center of block.

Block Eighteen~ Diagonal Pinwheels

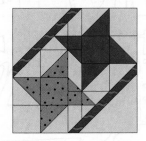

Fabrics for Block Eighteen

Tan - Two 4¾" squares
  Two 2½" x 5½" pieces
  Ten 2½" squares
  One 1½" x 3½" piece
  Four 1½" x 2½" pieces

Dark Red - Four 2½" squares
  Three 1½" squares

Lt Green - Four 2½" squares
  Three 1½" squares

Dark Green - Two 5½" squares

Making Block Eighteen

1. Refer to Making Quick Corner Triangles on page 92. Making a quick corner triangle, sew one 2½" dark red square to one 2½" tan square. Press. Make six, three with dark red and tan and three with light green and tan.

Red or Light Green = 2½" x 2½"
Tan = 2½" x 2½"
Make 6
(3 of each combination)

2. Arrange and sew one 2½" x 5½" tan piece, one unit from step 1, and one 2½" tan square. Press. Make two, one of each combination.

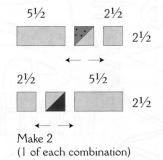

Make 2
(1 of each combination)

3. Making a quick corner triangle unit, sew one 1½" light green square to one 1½" x 2½" tan piece as shown. Press. Sew unit to one 2½" tan square as shown. Press. Make two, one of each combination as shown.

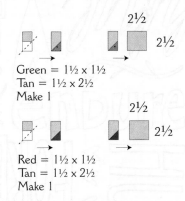

Green = 1½ x 1½
Tan = 1½ x 2½
Make 1

Red = 1½ x 1½
Tan = 1½ x 2½
Make 1

4. Arrange and sew two light green units from step 1, one 2½" light green square, and one dark red unit from step 3 as shown. Press. Make two, one of each combination as shown.

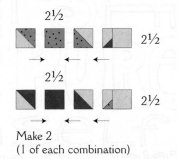

Make 2
(1 of each combination)

5. Making quick corner triangle units, sew one 1½" dark red square and one 1½" light green square to one 1½" x 3½" tan piece as shown. Press. Arrange and sew unit with two 1½" x 2½" tan pieces, one 1½" dark red square, and one 1½" light green square as shown. Press.

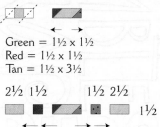

Green = 1½ x 1½
Red = 1½ x 1½
Tan = 1½ x 3½

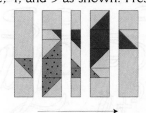

6. Arrange and sew units from steps 2, 4, and 5 as shown. Press.

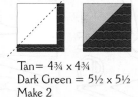

7. Making a quick corner triangle unit, sew one 4¾" tan square to one 5½" dark green square as shown. Press. Make two.

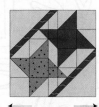

Tan = 4¾ x 4¾
Dark Green = 5½ x 5½
Make 2

8. Making quick corner triangle units, sew units from step 7 to unit from step 6 as shown. Prior to stitching, flip back unit to make sure of positioning. Press. Block Eighteen measures 9½" square.

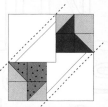

Unit from step 7
Unit from step 6

Block Eighteen measures 9½" square

Block Twenty~ You Glow Girl!

Fabrics for Block Twenty

Tan - Four 2½" x 5" pieces
Four 2½" x 3" pieces
Red - One 5½" square
Light Green - Four 3" squares
Dark Green - Eight 2" squares
Assorted Scraps for Appliqués
Lightweight Fusible Web - ¼ yard
Five Assorted Buttons

Making Block Twenty

1. Refer to Making Quick Corner Triangles on page 92. Sew four 3" light green squares to one 5½" red square as shown. Press.

Lt Green= 3 x 3
Red = 5½ x 5½

2. Making a quick corner triangle unit, sew one 2" dark green square to one 2½" x 3" tan piece as shown. Press. Make four, two of each variation. Sew units together in pairs as shown. Press. Make two.

Dark Green = 2 x 2½
Tan = 2½ x 36
Make 4
(2 of each variation)

Make 2

3. Sew unit from step 1 between two units from step 2 as shown. Press.

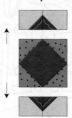

4. Making quick corner triangle units, sew one 2" dark green square to one 2½" x 5" tan piece as shown. Press. Make four, two of each variation. Sew units together in pairs as shown. Press. Make two.

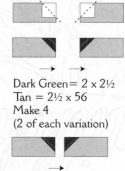

Dark Green= 2 x 2½
Tan = 2½ x 56
Make 4
(2 of each variation)

Make 2

5. Sew unit from step 3 between two units from step 4 as shown. Press. Block Twenty measures 9½" square.

Block Twenty measures 9½" square

6. Refer to Quick Fuse Appliqué on page 93. Use patterns on page 18 to trace one Glow Flower and four Small Glow Flower and Leaves. Use assorted scraps to prepare appliqués for fusing. Referring to block layout, position and fuse pieces to block. Finish appliqué edges with machine blanket stitch or other decorative stitching as desired. Add buttons to flower centers after quilting is completed.

Assembly

1. Refer to photo on page 4. Sew four blocks and three 2½" x 9½" sashing pieces to make a horizontal row. Press seams toward sashing. Make five rows.

2. Sew remaining sashing strips end-to-end to make one continuous 2½"-wide sashing strip. Measure rows in step 1 and cut six sashing strips to that measurement. Referring to photo on page 4, arrange and sew six sashing strips and five rows from step 1. Press.

3. Measure quilt through center from top to bottom. Cut two sashing strips to that measurement and sew to sides of quilt. Press.
Note: We chose a sashing fabric that was also used in the blocks. Blocks with the same color adjacent to the sashing were bordered with green rick rack to help them stand out

Adding the Borders

1. Sew 1" x 42" First Border strips end-to-end to make one continuous 1"-wide border strip. Press. Refer to Adding the Borders on page 94. Measure quilt through center from side to side. Cut two 1"-wide First Border strips to that measurement and sew to top and bottom of quilt. Press seams toward border.

2. Measure quilt through center from top to bottom including borders just added. Cut two 1"-wide First Border strips to that measurement. Sew to sides of quilt. Press.

3. Refer to steps 1 and 2 to join, measure, trim, and sew 1¼"-wide Second Border and 5"-wide Outside Border to top, bottom, and sides of quilt. Press seams toward border just sewn.

Layering and Finishing

1. Cut backing in half crosswise into two equal pieces. Sew pieces together to make one 66" x 80" (approximate) backing piece. Press.

2. Referring to Layering the Quilt on page 94, arrange and baste backing, batting, and top together.

3. Machine or hand quilt as desired.

4. Sew 2¾" x 42" binding strips end-to-end to make one continuous 2¾"-wide binding strip. Refer to Binding the Quilt on page 95 and bind quilt to finish.

5. Attach embellishments as desired.

Milestones

Celebration with Gratitude

So many people touch our lives along the way. In the past 20 years, I've been blessed to have many wonderful people come into my life as a result of my business. Anything that I've accomplished is thanks to talents, hard work, and dedication of the people I've surrounded myself with. Celebrating this milestone anniversary brings to the surface lots of memories and much gratitude for those that have shared this journey and this celebration with me.

Anniversary Quilt Patterns
Patterns are reversed for use with Quick-Fuse Appliqué (page 93).

Tracing Line ——————
Tracing Line -----------------
(will be hidden behind other fabrics)

Quilting Bee Pattern

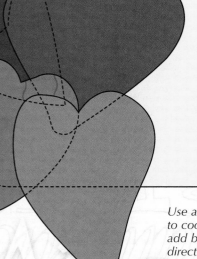

Use a favorite block for a pillow to coordinate with the quilt. Just add borders and finish following directions on page 95

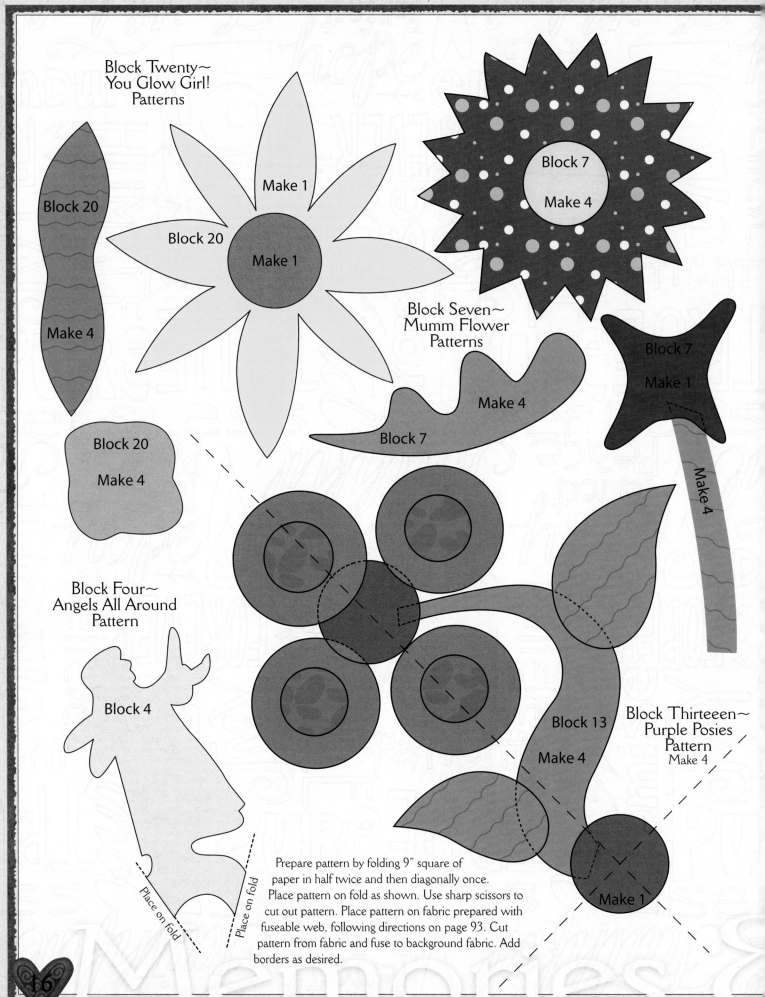

Block Twenty~
You Glow Girl!
Patterns

Block 20

Block 20

Make 1

Make 1

Block 20

Make 4

Block 20

Make 4

Block 7

Make 4

Block Seven~
Mumm Flower
Patterns

Make 4

Block 7

Block 7

Make 1

Make 4

Block Four~
Angels All Around
Pattern

Block 4

Block 13

Make 4

Block Thirteeen~
Purple Posies
Pattern
Make 4

Make 1

Place on fold

Place on fold

Prepare pattern by folding 9" square of paper in half twice and then diagonally once. Place pattern on fold as shown. Use sharp scissors to cut out pattern. Place pattern on fabric prepared with fuseable web, following directions on page 93. Cut pattern from fabric and fuse to background fabric. Add borders as desired.

Block Twelve~
Butterfly Whirl
Patterns

Block 12

Dark Petals

Make 4

Block 12

Leaf

Make 4

Block 12

Light Petals

Make 4

Block Two~
Playful Pansies
Pattern

Block 2

Anniversary Quilt Patterns

Patterns are reversed for use
with Quick-Fuse Appliqué (page 93).

Tracing Line ——————
Tracing Line ——————————
(will be hidden behind other fabrics)
Embroidery Line ···················
Placement Line — — — —

Block 17

Block
Seventeen~
Sunflower
Evolution Pattern

Swirl is couched yarn
~see page 95,
small circles denote
bead placement.

CAT'S CRADLE BLOCK (Block Eight) ~ Contributor: Wanda Jeffries

Machine quilting is an important part of many of Debbie's quilt designs and Wanda is a wizard at the long-arm machine. Wanda has been doing machine quilting for the Debbie Mumm Studio for seven years ...a challenge that she says "has helped me grow in my creativity." Her machine quilting work is as complex and fascinating as the classic block she chose to make for the Anniversary Quilt.
Instructions for Cat's Cradle begin on page 10.

SEWING CIRCLE BLOCK (Block Nine) ~ Contributor: Kelly Fisher

When Kelly first started working for Debbie in 1992, she assisted with quilt design, wrote pattern instructions, and drew piecing illustrations—by hand! When she left the company in 1999, she was Senior Editor working with three other designers in the sewing studio. A native Montanan, Kelly and her husband are avid motorcycle riders and recently moved into their country dream home in Fairfield, Washington, where she has a beautifully organized and functional sewing studio.
Instructions for Sewing Circle begin on page 11.

WHIMSICAL TEAPOT BLOCK (Block Ten) ~ Contributor: Jackie Saling

Decorative painter, fabric designer, master at crafts, product review manager—Jackie has done just about every job at the Debbie Mumm Studio except sew! After a career teaching decorative painting, Jackie went to work for Debbie more than ten years ago and is currently product review manager and fabric designer. She also designs and paints many of the projects in Debbie's books. When she isn't working, Jackie spends her time gardening, entertaining grandchildren, or soaking in her hot tub.
Whimsical Teapot Block features a painted teapot on a fabric background. Due to space limitations, pattern is not provided. Mix textile medium (available in craft stores) with acrylic craft paints in the proportion specified on the textile medium bottle, paint, allow to dry thoroughly, then set paint with a dry iron.

CROSSED PATHS BLOCK (Block Eleven) ~ Contributor: Retta Warehime

Retta and Debbie have been friends for nearly twenty years, ever since they worked together at the Quilting Bee in Spokane. Mother of four and a grandmother, Retta and her family have hosted many hockey players over the years. "Debbie was my inspiration to publish and design," says Retta, who is the author of five quilting books and is working on a new fabric line.
Instructions for Crossed Paths begin on page 11.

BUTTERFLY WHIRL BLOCK (Block Twelve) ~ Contributor: Roberta Rose-Knauth

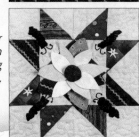

A life-long quilter, Roberta worked in Debbie's design studio in the 90's as a quilt and craft designer and dollmaker. She now runs her own quilt shop and design company in North Idaho and does custom long-arm quilting. While sitting in a garden in Skagway, Alaska, Roberta saw a group of butterflies dancing around one big lovely flower. This reminded her of her favorite childhood square dance, the Butterfly Whirl, and was the inspiration for this block.
Instructions for Butterfly Whirl begin on page 12. Applique patterns for Butterfly Whirl are on page 17.

PURPLE POSIES BLOCK (Block Thirteen) ~ Contributor: Candy Huddleston

A creative and unconventional quilter, Candy loves to work with bright colors and unusual designs in her quilts. Candy took her first quilting class in 1982 while in the Air Force, then settled in Spokane and has been active with Washington State Quilters for nearly two decades, including being honored as featured quilter at the 2004 Quilt Show. Candy worked as a seamstress in Debbie's Sewing Studio for five years. Currently she works for Spokane Public Library and shares her quilts with occasional displays at the libraries.
Applique patterns for Purple Posies are on page 18. Cut petals and leaves with pinking shears and sew approximately ⅛ " from cut edge to anchor to block. Candy "fussy-cut" flower centers and leaves so the fabric elements become an essential part of her design.

CUPPA COFFEE BLOCK (Block Fourteen) ~ Contributor Mya Brooks

A former production director for Debbie's company, Mya currently uses her vast organizational skills to balance working for Whitworth College, studying for her teaching certification, and taking care of her home and family. Even with her busy schedule, she still finds some time for her favorite hobbies—sewing and scrapbooking.
Cuppa Coffee Block features an embroidered center motif. Look for design ideas in clip art CDs and booklets. A log cabin style border finishes this block. Due to space limitations, embroidery patterns are not included.

THE CAT'S MEOW BLOCK (Block Fifteen) ~ Contributor: Jean Van Bockel

Debbie has a cat with a notoriously loud "meow" so it's no surprise that Jean would select a cat motif for her block. This animal lover has worked for Debbie as a quilt and craft designer and is the author of several books published by Martingale & Company. Accompanied by her dogs, Jean finds inspiration for quilt designs during long rambles through the woods near her Northern Idaho home.
Due to space limitations, appliqué pattern is not included.

HEARTS AND FLOWER BLOCK (Block Sixteen) ~ Contributor Heather Butler

Known for her off-beat sense of humor and eclectic music collection, Heather has worked for Debbie as an artist and graphics designer for six years. An accomplished designer, Heather's needlework has been featured in several publications. She and her husband enjoy finding new ways to make their toddler son laugh.
The Hearts and Flower Block has a four-patch background with embroidery designs on the light blocks. Due to space limitations, embroidery patterns are not included.

SUNFLOWER EVOLUTION BLOCK (Block Seventeen) ~ Contributor: Carolyn Ogden

As managing editor of Debbie's publications, Carolyn enjoys being part of the evolution of Debbie's books, artwork, and fabric designs. A writer and public relations professional, Carolyn was able to turn her flair for sewing, craft, and decorating into her profession when she joined the Debbie Mumm team. Known for her ebullient laugh, Carolyn is a notorious bargain-hunter who loves garage sales and flea markets and will "negotiate" with anyone.
Applique patterns for Sunflower Evolution are on page 17. Strip-pieced, crazy quilt-style borders surround the central motif. Quick-fuse appliqué was finished with hand blanket stitching on this block. Couched chenille yarn and beads embellish the sunflower center.

DIAGONAL PINWHEELS BLOCK (Block Eighteen) ~ Contributor: Jodi Gosse

Jodi and Debbie share a unique bond—Jodi adopted Debbie's dog! Jodi worked in the Mumm Studio for five years until her family (including the dog!) moved back to Illinois. As Jodi says, "we worked hard, yet had a lot of fun and shared a lot of laughter." Mother of three grown sons, Jodi is the manager of a community center, and continues to quilt in her spare time.
Instructions for Diagonal Pinwheel begin on page 16.

FIDDLESTICKS BLOCK (Block Nineteen) ~ Contributor: Michelle Sink

"The Voguest girls in town" was the description for Debbie, Michelle, and the staff at Fiddlesticks, the shop where Debbie got her start in quilting. Debbie and Michelle were co-workers at Fiddlesticks when Debbie took her first quilting class, and as Michelle says, "the rest is history!" Michelle is now president and owner of the home accessories and gift shop.
A photo transfer technique is a great way to add a memorable photograph to a quilt. Check with your local quilt shop for products and tips. A log cabin method finishes the Fiddlesticks Block.

YOU GLOW GIRL! BLOCK (Block Twenty) ~ Contributor: Carolyn Golden Lowe

A former Home Ec teacher, Carolyn has worked with Debbie for six years as a quilt designer. This native Tennessean is our resident expert on machine embroidery techniques and the go-to girl for sewing and cooking questions. Carolyn and husband Ted live on a lovely Christmas tree farm near Mount Spokane and enjoy the natural beauty while trying to keep a garden growing despite frequent visits from deer and wild turkeys. A historic cabin on their property has been a photo location for three of Debbie's books.
Instructions for You Glow Girl! begin on page 14. Appliqué patterns for You Glow Girl! are on page 16.

QUILTING BEE PILLOW ~ Contributor: Jackie Wolff

The owner of the Quilting Bee in Spokane, Washington, Jackie's encouragement and assistance were instrumental in Debbie's decision to form her quilting design company. It was Jackie who prompted Debbie to pack up her handful of patterns and get on an airplane for the first time in her life to go to International Quilt Market. Wearing her signature overalls and with her bright smile, Jackie is an important part of the quilting industry in Spokane and a true friend.
Appliqué patterns for the Quilting Bee are on page 15. Jackie hand-finished the edges with a blanket stitch and added bee and spool buttons and embroidered accents. This block was used for our matching pillow.

When a baby arrives...

...it's a time of **great joy**.
Baby giggles and cuddly quilts, crocheted bears
and tiny shirts, purple elephants and little ears are all
expressions of celebration in the
circle of **friends and family**.

Creating a nursery spans the emotions
of excitement for the **expectant** to
creating a **calming and cozy**
environment for baby to fall asleep.

Combine fleece and cottons for a **snuggly**
quilt to welcome and wrap
the new little one in
love and goodness.

This cuddly keepsake will
bring back memories of
those fleeting **baby days** in
years to come.

Cuddles Crib Quilt

Fleece and cotton combine to make a soft, cuddly, and cute quilt for baby. Stars and moon printed fleece was fussy-cut for several of the blocks and borders, but we also provide appliqué patterns if you wish to add the stars and moon with an appliqué technique.

Cuddles Crib Quilt 49" x 63"	FIRST CUT		SECOND CUT	
	Number of Strips or Pieces	Dimensions	Number of Pieces	Dimensions
Fabric A Block 1 Borders & Purple Blocks 1/3 yard	1	7½" x 42"	2	7½" squares
			8	7½" x 1¾"
	1	1¾" x 42"	8	1¾" x 5"
Fabric B Centers for Blocks 1, 2, 3 1/3 yard	2	5" x 42"	12	5" squares
Fabric C Block 2 Borders & Block 4 ¼ yard	1	7½" x 42"	1	7½" square (Block 4)
			8	7½" x 1¾"
			8	5" x 1¾"
Fabric D Block 3 Borders ¼ yard	3	1¾" x 42"	8	1¾" x 7½"
			8	1¾" x 5"
Fabric E Yellow Blocks ¼ yard	1	7½" x 42"	5	7½" squares
Fabric F Fleece Block ¼ yard	1	7½" x 42"	4	7½" squares (fussy cut)
Fabric G Light Green Blocks ¼ yard	1	7½" x 42"	4	7½" squares
Fabric H Lavender Blocks ¼ yard	1	7½" x 42"	3	7½" squares
Fabric I Fleece Blocks ¼ yard	1	7½" x 42"	4	7½" squares (fussy cut)
BORDERS				
Accent Border ¼ yard	5	1½" x 42"		
Outside Border 2¼ yards (60" Fleece) OR 1⅛ yards (42" Cotton)	4	6" x 60" (fussy cut)		
	6	6" x 42"		
Binding ⅝ yard	6	3" x 42" **OR**		
	6	2¾" x 42" (for use with cotton backing)		

Backing - 2 yards of 60"-wide fabric OR 3⅛ yards of 45"-wide fabric
Batting - 54" x 68" (optional)
Moon & Star Appliqués - Assorted Scraps
Tear-Away Stabilizer
Temporary Spray Adhesive
Black Embroidery Floss (optional)

Fabric and Cutting Requirements

Read all instructions before beginning and use ¼"-wide seam allowances throughout. Read Cutting Strips and Pieces on page 92 prior to cutting fabrics.

Getting Started

This quilt consists of thirty-five blocks, each measuring 7½" square unfinished. Twelve blocks are pieced and then embellished with "fussy cut" fleece star appliqués; one block is embellished with a "fussy cut" moon appliqué. For added warmth and softness, we used fleece for several blocks, the Outside Border, and backing. Since the backing is fleece, we eliminated the batting and used wider-than-usual cotton binding strips to compensate for the thickness of two layers of fleece. If you prefer to use batting and a cotton backing, however, we've included those requirements in the cutting chart.

Refer to Accurate Seam Allowance on page 92. Whenever possible, use the Assembly Line Method on page 92. Press seams in direction of arrows.

Blocks

Note: Use extra care when pressing fleece, or finger press only.

1. Sew one 5" Fabric B square between two 1¾" x 5" Fabric A pieces as shown. Press. Make four.

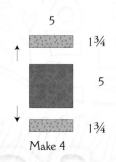

Make 4

2. Sew one unit from step 1 between two 7½" x 1¾" Fabric A pieces as shown. Press. Make four and label Block 1. Block 1 measures 7½" square.

Block 1

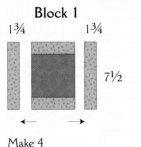

1¾   1¾

7½

Make 4
Block 1 measures 7½" square

3. Sew one 5" Fabric B square between two 5" x 1¾" Fabric C pieces as shown. Press. Make four.

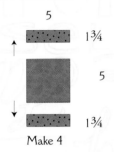

5

1¾

5

1¾

Make 4

4. Sew one unit from step 3 between two 7½" x 1¾" Fabric C pieces as shown. Press. Make four and label Block 2. Block 2 measures 7½" square.

Block 2

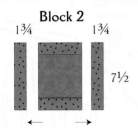

1¾   1¾

7½

Make 4
Block 2 measures 7½" square

5. Sew one 5" Fabric B square between two 1¾" x 5" Fabric D pieces as shown. Press. Make four.

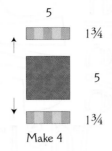

5

1¾

5

1¾

Make 4

6. Sew one unit from step 5 between two 1¾" x 7½" Fabric D pieces as shown. Press. Make four and label Block 3. Block 3 measures 7½" square.

Block 3

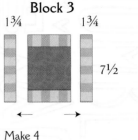

1¾   1¾

7½

Make 4
Block 3 measures 7½" square

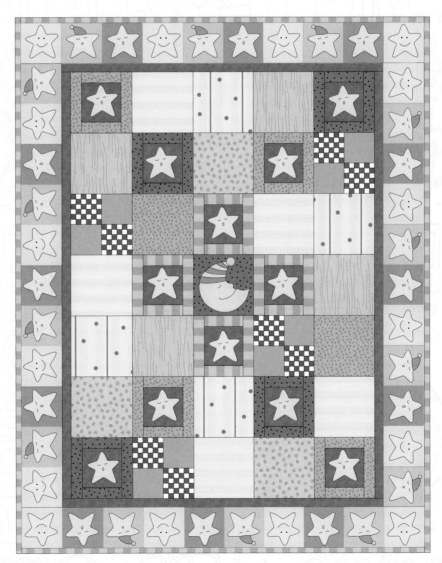

Cuddles Crib Quilt
Finished Size: 49" x 63"

23

Memories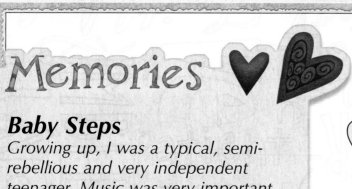

Baby Steps

Growing up, I was a typical, semi-rebellious and very independent teenager. Music was very important me. I remember one year at Christmas there was a big, bulky package under the tree with my name on it. I was certain it was going to be the stereo that I wanted so badly. To my disappointment, not only wasn't it a stereo…it was a SEWING MACHINE! Of course, in hindsight, what a really good thing that was.

One thing I've learned over time and through experience, you don't always recognize the significance of an event at the moment it is happening.

Cuddles Crib Quilt Patterns

Patterns are reversed for use with Quick-Fuse Appliqué (page 93).

Tracing Line _____
Tracing Line _ _ _ _ _ _ _ _ _ _ _ _
(will be hidden behind other fabrics)
Embroidery Lines....................

7. Refer to Machine Appliqué on page 93 eliminating step 1. Refer to photo on page 20 and layout on page 23. Use temporary spray adhesive to position one "fussy cut" fleece star on each of Blocks 1, 2, and 3. Position and adhere "fussy cut" fleece moon to 7½" Fabric C square. Place tear-away stabilizer on back of blocks and finish appliqué edges with machine blanket stitch or other decorative stitching as desired. Label Moon block Block 4.

OR

Refer to Quick-Fuse Appliqué on page 93. Use patterns on page 24 to make templates for moon (including all night cap pieces) and star. Use assorted scraps to trace and cut one moon and twelve stars. Refer to photo on page 20 and layout on page 23 to position and fuse one star to each of Blocks 1, 2, and 3. Position and fuse moon to 7½" Fabric C square and label Block 4. Finish appliqué edges with machine blanket stitch or other decorative stitching as desired.

Refer to Embroidery Stitch Guide on page 95 and use two strands of black embroidery floss and a stem stitch to embroider eyes and mouths on stars and moon.

Block 1   Block 2   Block 3

Block 4
7½

7½

Assembly

Refer to photo on page 20 and diagram below. Arrange and sew Blocks 1, 2, 3, 4, and 7½" squares of Fabric A, E, F, G, H and I in seven horizontal rows of five blocks each. Press seams in opposite directions from row to row. Sew rows together. Press.

Block 1	E	F	G	Block 2
G	Block 2	H	Block 1	I
I	A	Block 3	E	F
E	Block 3	Block 4	Block 3	G
F	G	Block 3	I	A
H	Block 1	F	Block 2	E
Block 2	I	E	H	Block 1

Borders

1. Sew 1½" Accent Border strips together end-to-end to make one continuous 1½"-wide border strip. Press. Measure quilt through center from top to bottom. Cut two 1½"-wide Accent Border strips to this measurement. Sew to sides of quilt. Press seams toward border.

2. Measure quilt through center from side to side including borders just added. Cut two 1½"-wide Accent Border strips to this measurement. Sew to top and bottom of quilt. Press.

3. For fleece Outside Borders, measure quilt through center from top to bottom. Cut two 6"-wide Outside Border strips to this measurement. Sew to sides of quilt. Press seams toward First Border.

Measure quilt through center from side to side including borders just added. Cut two 6"-wide Outside Border strips to this measurement. Sew to top and bottom of quilt. Press.

OR

For cotton Outside Borders, refer to steps 1 and 2 to join, measure, trim and sew 6"-wide Outside Border strips to sides, top, and bottom of quilt. Press seams toward newly added borders.

Layering and Finishing

For fleece backing (60"-wide fabric):

1. Arrange and baste backing and top together referring to Layering the Quilt on page 94. Machine or hand quilt as desired. Use a walking foot for machine quilting to prevent stretching of fleece.

2. Sew 3"-wide binding strips end-to-end to make one continuous 3"-wide binding strip. Trim backing to ¼" beyond edge of quilt top. Refer to Binding the Quilt on page 95 and bind quilt to finish.

For cotton backing (45"-wide fabric):

1. Cut backing in half crosswise into two equal pieces. Sew pieces together lengthwise to make one 56" x 80" (approximate) backing piece. Press and trim backing to 56 " x 68".

2. Arrange and baste backing, batting, and top together referring to Layering the Quilt on page 94. Hand or machine quilt as desired.

3. Sew 2¾"-wide binding strips end-to-end to make one continuous 2¾"-wide binding strip. Refer to Binding the Quilt on page 95 and bind quilt to finish.

Childhood Memories...

...are a powerful **influence on the future**. Providing a colorful and **creative environment** for a child is a great way to **inspire** imaginative play and **creativity**.

With their strong colors and geometric designs, these colorful quilts pave the way for creative **play** and provide an everyday **teaching** tool for colors and shapes.

Quilting provides **design and texture** to the projects adding another **layer of learning** to this dynamic setting.

Paint Box Bed Quilt

Create a colorful and creative environment for your child. Easy strip-piecing and quick corner triangles make this quilt a fast and easy project. A rainbow of vibrant colors is softened by touches of tan, making this quilt a happy addition to a child's room. Fanciful quilting with variegated thread adds fabulous texture and even more fun to this child-right quilt.

Paint Box Bed Quilt 72" x 96"		FIRST CUT		SECOND CUT	
		Number of Strips or Pieces	Dimensions	Number of Pieces	Dimensions
	Fabric A Green Strip 1 yard	12	2½" x 42"		
	Fabric B Purple Strip 1 yard	12	2½" x 42"		
	Fabric C Orange Strip 1 yard	12	2½" x 42"		
	Fabric D Blue Strip 1 yard	12	2½" x 42"		
	Fabric E Red Strip 1 yard	12	2½" x 42"		
	Fabric F Yellow Strip 1 yard	12	2½" x 42"		
	Fabric G Corners 2¼ yards	12	6½" x 42"	70	6½" squares
BORDERS					
	First Border ⅜ yard	8	1½" x 42"		
	Outside Border 1⅙ yards	8	5" x 42"		
	Binding ¾ yard	9	2¾" x 42"		
Backing - 6⅔ yards Batting - 80" x 104"					

Fabric Requirements and Cutting Instructions

Read all instructions before beginning and use ¼"-wide seam allowances throughout. Read Cutting Strips and Pieces on page 92 prior to cutting fabric.

Getting Started

This quilt consists of thirty-five blocks measuring 12½" square (unfinished). Efficient strip piecing and Quick Corner Triangles make the blocks easy to assemble. All blocks use the same fabrics, but strips are arranged in different orders to make six variations. Note the order of strips and the orientation of blocks when placing in the quilt.

This quilt has an added benefit: a smaller wall version and a mini quilt you can make with the leftovers.

Refer to Accurate Seam Allowance on page 92. Whenever possible, use the Assembly Line Method on page 92. Press seams in direction of arrows.

Blocks

1. Arrange and sew together one each of 2½" x 42" Fabric A, B, C, D, E, and F strips as shown to make a strip set. Press. Make two.

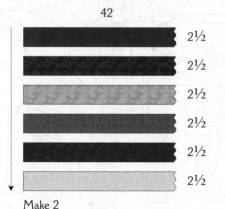

42

2½
2½
2½
2½
2½
2½

Make 2

2. Cut six 12½"
   segments from strip
   sets as shown.

12½   12½

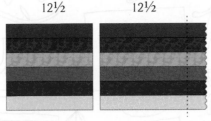

Cut 6 segments

3. Refer to Quick Corner Triangles on page 92. Sew two 6½"
   Fabric G squares to one unit from step 2 as shown. Press.
   Make six and label Block A.

Block 1

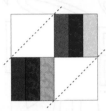 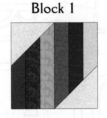

G = 6½ x 6½
Unit from step 2

←   →

Make 6
Block measures 12½" x 12½"

Paint Box Bed Quilt
Finished Size: 72" x 96"

✳Milestones

Learning Curve
*In the early 80's, I moved from
Seattle to a small town in central
Washington. At the time, I dreaded
the move, but it turned out to be
a significant crossroads for me. I
started working in a cute little
shop named Fiddlesticks. Half
of the store was gifts and home
decor and half was quilting. I
loved the environment and all
the "stuff," but knew nothing
about the quilting side. So I took
my first quilting class and made my
first quilt, a Double Irish Chain. I
was completely intrigued. Once I
understood how to construct a quilt,
I was itching to start designing my
own... and that's the very next thing
I did. The second quilt I ever made
was one I designed. I named it
"Heart's Content."*

4. Referring to steps 1 and 2 and diagrams below, use remaining 2½" x 42" strips to make two matching strip sets for each combination as shown, noting placement of color. Press. Cut twenty-nine 12½" segments, six of four combinations and five of one combination from remaining pairs of strip sets. Label units 2, 3, 4, 5, and 6 as shown.

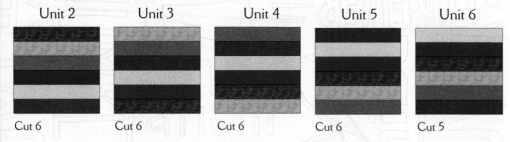

Unit 2	Unit 3	Unit 4	Unit 5	Unit 6
Cut 6	Cut 6	Cut 6	Cut 6	Cut 5

5. Making quick corner triangle units, sew two 6½" Fabric G squares to each unit from step 4 as shown. Press. Make twenty-nine blocks, six of combinations B, C, D, and E, and five of combination F. Label each combination. Blocks measure 12½" square.

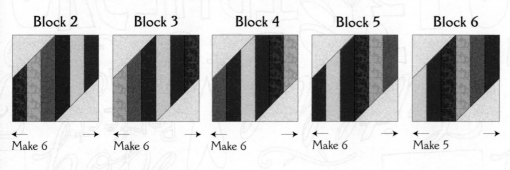

Block 2	Block 3	Block 4	Block 5	Block 6
← Make 6 →	← Make 6 →	← Make 6 →	← Make 6 →	← Make 5 →

Assembly

Refer to photo on page 26 and layout on page 29. Arrange and sew seven horizontal rows of five blocks each, noting placement of colors and direction of triangles. Press seams in opposite directions from row to row. Arrange and sew rows together. Press.

1	2	3	4	5
2	3	4	5	6
3	4	5	6	1
4	5	6	1	2
5	6	1	2	3
6	1	2	3	4
1	2	3	4	5

Borders

1. Refer to Adding the Borders on page 94. Sew 1½" x 42" First Border strips together end-to-end to make one continuous 1½"-wide First Border strip. Press. Measure quilt through center from side to side. Cut two 1½"-wide First Border strips to this measurement. Sew to top and bottom of quilt. Press seams toward border.

2. Measure quilt through center from top to bottom including borders just added. Cut two 1½"-wide First Border strips to this measurement. Sew to sides of quilt. Press.

3. Refer to steps 1 and 2 to join, measure, trim, and sew 5"-wide Outside Border strips to top, bottom, and sides of quilt. Press.

Layering and Finishing

1. Cut backing crosswise into three equal pieces. Sew pieces together lengthwise to make one 80" x 120" (approximate) backing piece. Press and trim to 80" x 104".

2. Arrange and baste backing, batting, and top together referring to Layering the Quilt on page 94.

3. Machine or hand quilt as desired.

4. Sew 2¾" x 42" binding strips end-to-end to make one continuous 2¾"-wide strip. Refer to Binding the Quilt on page 95 and bind quilt to finish.

Paint Box Pillows

Assorted Sizes

Accent the Paint Box Quilt with these clever and colorful pillows that add dimension and geometry to a room. Buttons in contrasting shapes and colors add fun detail.

Materials Needed

Circle Pillow

Orange Pillow Tops & Gusset -
⅝ yard
   Two 14½" circles
   Two 3" x 42" strips

Batting & Lining - Two 17"
   squares for each

Polyester Fiberfil

Two Square Blue Buttons

Square Pillow

Green Pillow Tops & Gusset - ¾
yard
   Two 17½" squares
   Two 3" x 42" strips

Batting & Lining - Two 20"
   squares for each

Polyester Fiberfil

Two Orange Triangular Buttons

Triangle Pillow

Purple Pillow Tops & Gusset - ⅝
yard
   Two equilateral triangles (each
   side 14" long)
   Two 3" x 42" fabric strips

Batting & Lining - Two 16"
   triangles for each

Polyester Fiberfil

Two Round Yellow Buttons

Getting Started

These simple, geometric pillows are sewn, turned, and stuffed. The quilting mimics the shape of each pillow for a subtle effect. Contrasting geometric buttons finish the design. Instructions for each pillow are the same, only the shapes and sizes vary.

Making the Pillows

1. For each pillow, layer batting piece between lining and pillow top fabric. Baste. Machine or hand quilt from center of pillow in a spiral-type motion imitating the shape of pillow top. Trim batting and lining even with raw edge of pillow top. Make two.

2. Sew matching 3" x 42" fabric strips together to make one 3"-wide strip. Press. Fabric strip sizes for each pillow are as follows: Circle pillow–3" x 44½", Square pillow–3" x 68½", and Triangle pillow–3" x 42½". Sew short ends of each strip together to make a circular strip (gussets). Press. Make three.

3. With right sides together, pin and sew fabric gusset from step 2 to matching pillow top. If this is a new skill for you, it is recommended that the gusset be basted first. For square and triangular pillows, pivot at corners.

4. Pin and sew remaining matching quilted section to unit from step 3 leaving a 4" opening for turning and stuffing and anchoring ends of stitching.

5. Turn pillow right side out, stuff as desired with fiberfill, and hand-stitch opening closed.

6. Using a long piece of doubled thread, attach buttons to each side of pillow, sewing through pillow and buttons, and pulling thread to create a slight depression in pillow top. Tie off thread under button.

Paint Box Wall Quilt

Finished Size: 44"x59"

Waste not, want not. With just a little extra yardage, this vibrant wall quilt can be created from the Quick Corner Triangle scraps from the Paint Box Bed Quilt. The striking geometric design and dramatic color scheme make it a focal point of the room

Materials Needed

Option 1: Trimmed corner triangle units from Paint Box Bed Quilt, page 28 **OR**

Option 2: ⅓ yard each of six fabrics in assorted colors, each fabric cut into three 2½"-wide strips.

Black Fabric - 1⅛ yards
   Thirty-five 6½" squares

First Border - ⅓ yard
   Five 1½" x 42" strips

Outside Border - ⅝ yard
   Five 3½" x 42" strips

Binding - ⅝ yard
   Six 2¾" x 42" strips

Backing - 3 yards

Batting - 50" x 65"

Getting Started

This quilt can be made easily using the strip-pieced portions trimmed from the blocks of the Paint Box Bed Quilt and by adding a few fabrics. Skip to step 3 if using Paint Box scraps, .

Assembly

Note: Follow steps 1 and step 2 **only** if you did not make Paint Box Bed Quilt on page 28. Otherwise skip to step 3.

1. Referring to photo and diagram below, sew together one each of three different-colored 2½"-wide fabric strips to make a strip set as shown. Press. Make six strip sets in assorted colors. Cut strip sets into thirty-five 6½"-wide segments as shown.

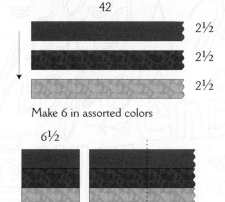

Cut 35 segments

2. Draw diagonal line on wrong side of one 6½" segment from step 1. Place marked unit and one 6½" black square right sides together. Sew scant ¼" away from drawn line on both sides to make half-square triangles as shown. Make thirty-five. Cut on drawn line. Press. This will make seventy half-square-triangle blocks. Square Blocks to 5½". Skip to step 4.

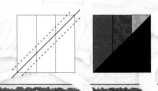

3. Assemble corner units trimmed from Paint Box Bed Quilt blocks, steps 3 and 5, on pages 29 and 30. With right sides together place two Paint Box units on one 6½" Black square matching corner edges as shown (Paint Box units will not completely cover square; there will be a gap in center). Sew ¼" from diagonal edges as shown. Make thirty-five sets. Trim as shown, leaving ¼"-wide seam allowances. Press. Square unit to 5½". This will make seventy half-square triangle blocks.

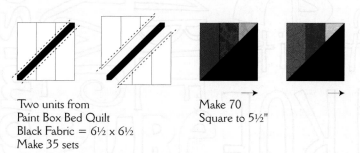

Two units from
Paint Box Bed Quilt
Black Fabric = 6½ x 6½
Make 35 sets

Make 70
Square to 5½"

4. Referring to photo, arrange and sew ten horizontal rows of seven blocks each. Press seams in opposite directions from row to row. Sew rows together. Press.

Borders

1. Refer to Adding the Borders on page 94. Measure quilt through center from side to side. Cut two 1½" x 42" First Border strips to this measurement. Sew to top and bottom of quilt. Press seams toward border.

2. Sew remaining 1½" x 42" First Border strips together end-to-end to make one continuous 1½"-wide border strip. Press. Measure quilt through center from top to bottom including borders just added. Cut two 1½"-wide First Border strips to this measurement. Sew to sides of quilt. Press.

3. Refer to steps 1 and 2 to measure, trim, and sew 3½"-wide Outside Border strips to top, bottom, and sides of quilt. Press.

Layering and Finishing

1. Cut backing in half crosswise into two equal pieces. Sew pieces together lengthwise to make one 54" x 80" (approximate) backing piece. Press and trim backing to 54" x 65".

2. Arrange and baste backing, batting, and top together referring to Layering the Quilt on page 94. Machine or hand quilt as desired.

3. Sew 2¾" x 42" binding strips end-to-end to make one continuous 2¾"-wide binding strip. Refer to Binding the Quilt on page 95 and bind quilt to finish.

Milestones

The Big Leap

After designing several quilts, I began teaching classes in my designs. Soon peers were encouraging me to put my designs into patterns and sell them. I spent a couple of years in research and development, and, in 1985, moved to Spokane, WA. where I went to work for The Quilting Bee.

In the fall of 1986, the quilt shop owner was heading to Houston, Texas, to attend the International Quilt Market tradeshow. Up until then, I'd never even heard of such a thing! With the support of the quilt shop, my friends and family, I made the decision to exhibit and introduce my line of patterns.

In May 1986, at the age of 30, I got on an airplane for the very first time and took the leap into the national quilting marketplace.

Going off to College...

...Is a major crossroad in a young adult's
life and a **giant step** toward independence.
For the first time, the student is **on her own**,
but still wants and needs the
comforts of home.

A colorful and inviting quilt for her bed
will **warm up** even the most austere
dorm room. Bold primary colors and an
enticing design make this quilt both a
great decorating piece and a warm
reminder of home.

The matching laundry bag features a
personalized monogram and will help
her stay **organized and tidy**.

In years to come, the quilt will move
beautifully into her first place and be a
constant **reminder** of her fun college
days and her **loving family** at home.

Off to College Bed Quilt

Mark a milestone step for your grown child or grandchild with a warm and colorful quilt that will be a loving reminder of home. This bed-sized quilt will decorate a dorm room with style and remind your newly-independent student of his supportive and loving family. With its clean-lined geometry, bright sashing, and unusual "woven ribbon" border, this twin bed-sized quilt is quick and easy to make between graduation parties and summer activities.

Off to College Bed Quilt 63" x 87"	FIRST CUT		SECOND CUT	
	Number of Strips or Pieces	Dimensions	Number of Pieces	Dimensions
Fabric A Four-Patch & Second Border 1⅛ yards	6 7	4½" x 42" 1" x 42" (Border)	48	4½" squares
Fabric B Four-Patch ⅞ yard	6	4½" x 42"	48	4½" squares
Fabric C Cross Pieces in Four Patch & Outside Border 2⅓ yards*	4 6 10	6½" x 42" (Border) 4½" x 42" 2½" x 42" (Border)	52 96	6½" x 2½"* 4½" x 2½"*
Fabric D Block Center & Outside Border ⅝ yard	7	2½" x 42" (5 strips are for border)	24	2½" squares
Fabric E Sashing & First Border 1¼ yards	12 6	2½" x 42" 2" x 42" (Border)	18	2½" x 10½"
Binding ¾ yards	8	2¾" x 42"		

Backing - 5⅙ yards
Batting - 71" x 93"
*For directional fabric, the size that is listed first runs parallel to selvage.

Fabric Requirements and Cutting Instructions

Read all instructions before beginning and use ¼"-wide seam allowances throughout. Read Cutting Strips and Pieces on page 92 prior to cutting fabric.

Getting Started

This quilt consists of twenty-four simple Four-Patch Blocks, with sashing, measuring 10½" square unfinished. The pieced border gives a woven ribbon effect that can be further enhanced by quilting around the "ribbon" pieces. This is a very easy quilt to make but it is important to sew an accurate ¼"-wide seam allowance since the border is pieced to the inside quilt dimensions. Directional fabric is used in the Blocks and Outside Border.

Refer to Accurate Seam Allowance on page 92. Whenever possible, use the Assembly Line method on page 92. Press seams in directions of arrows.

Making the Blocks

1. Sew one 4½" x 2½" Fabric C piece between one 4½" Fabric A square and one 4½" Fabric B square as shown. Press. Make forty-eight.

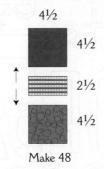

Make 48

2. Sew one 2½" Fabric D square between two 4½" x 2½" Fabric C pieces as shown. Press. Make twenty-four.

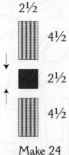

Make 24

3. Sew one unit from step 2 between two units from step 1 as shown. Press. Make twenty-four Four-Patch Blocks. Block measures 10½" square.

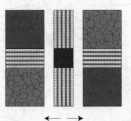

Make 24
Block measures 10½" square

Assembly

1. Sew together three 2½" x 10½" Fabric E pieces and four Four-Patch Blocks to make a row, checking orientation of Blocks as shown. Press. Make six rows. Row measures 10½" x 46½".

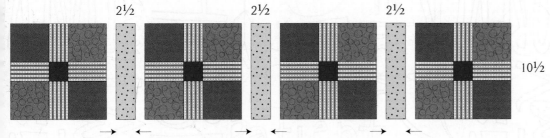

Make 6 rows

2. Sew six 2½" x 42" Fabric E strips end-to-end to make one continuous 2½"-wide strip. From this strip cut five 2½" x 46½" sashing strips.

3. Referring to layout, arrange and sew five strips from step 2 between the six rows from step 1. Press seams toward sashing.

Borders

1. Sew 2" x 42" Fabric E strips end-to-end to make one continuous 2"-wide strip. From this strip cut two 2" x 73½" and two 2" x 46½" First Border strips.

2. Arrange and sew 2" x 46½" strips to top and bottom of quilt. Press seams toward Border. Sew 2" x 73½" strips to sides. Press.

3. Sew 1" x 42" Fabric A strips end-to-end to make one continuous 1"-wide strip. From this strip cut two 1" x 74½" and two 1" x 49½" Fabric A Second Border strips.

4. Arrange and sew 1" x 49½" strips to top and bottom of quilt. Press seams toward border. Sew 1" x 74½" strips to sides. Press.

Off to College Bed Quilt
Finished Size: 63" x 87"

Memories

Penguins are Popular!

One of the most favorite little fellas in my life has been this playful penguin! Mummford® sprang to life in 1998 and became a major celebrity through lots of promotion by Mervyn's Department Stores. Mummford appeared on hundreds of products in a full store promotion for Christmas 1998 and 1999. Children's books, ornaments, t-shirts, pajamas, and many more items included Mummford's image. Mummford was on the set of many prime-time TV shows and became a regular on the "Friends" television show, when Joey adopted the plush penguin and named him "Hugsy." To this day, Mummford is still the subject of bidding wars on E-bay and one of my most popular products.

Pieced Outside Border

1. Sew one 2½" x 42" Fabric D strip between two 2½" x 42" Fabric C strips to make a strip set as shown. Press. Make five. Cut forty 4½"-wide segments and four 2½"-wide segments.

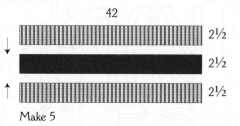
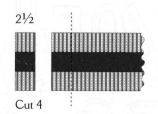

2. Sew together eight 4½"-wide segments from step 1 between nine 6½" x 2½" Fabric C pieces as shown. Press. Make two rows. Row measures 6½" x 50½".

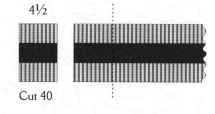

Make 2 rows

3. Arrange and sew units from step 2 to top and bottom of quilt. Press seams toward Second Border.

4. Sew one 2½"-wide segment from step 1 between two 6½" x 2½" Fabric C pieces as shown. Press. Make four. Block measures 6½"-square.

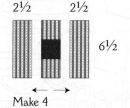

Make 4
Block measures 6½" square

5. Arrange and sew twelve 4½"-wide segments from step 1 between thirteen 6½" x 2½" Fabric C pieces. Press. Make two. Sew row between two units from step 4 as shown. Press. Make two. Row measures 6½" x 74½".

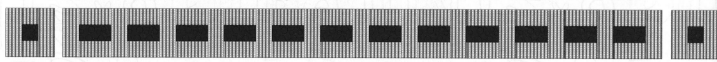

Make 2

6. Arrange and sew rows from step 5 to sides of quilt. Press seams toward Second Border.

Layering & Finishing

1. Cut backing crosswise into two equal pieces. Sew pieces together lengthwise to make one 80" x 93" (approximate) backing piece. Press and trim to 71" x 93".

2. Arrange and baste backing, batting, and top together, referring to Layering the Quilt on page 94.

3. Hand or machine quilt as desired.

4. Sew 2¾" x 42" binding strips end-to-end to make one continuous 2¾"-wide strip. Refer to Binding the Quilt on page 95 and bind quilt to finish.

Off to College Laundry Bag

Finished Size: 20" x 34"
As bright and colorful as it is functional, this laundry bag will make life a little easier for a college-bound student. The large size, a toggle-style drawstring, and a cool monogram make this laundry bag a useful dorm accessory.

Materials Needed

Fabric A - 1⅛ yard
　　One 40½" x 36" piece
Fabric B - ¼ yard
　　One 40½" x 6½" strip
Fabric C - Scrap, one 6" x 9" piece
Cording - 1½ yards
Cord Lock
Embroidery Thread or Floss

Making the Laundry Bag

1. Turn under ¼" hem on both long sides of 40½" x 6½" Fabric B strip. Press.

2. Position pressed Fabric B strip 12" down from top edge of 40½" x 36" Fabric A piece and edge stitch as shown.

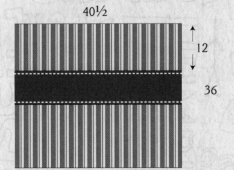

40½

12

36

3. The monogram is embroidered on the 6" x 9" Fabric C piece. We used London font and Bernina® Artista 200E machine. If you prefer hand embroidery, refer to Embroidery Stitch Guide on page 95. Choose lettering by selecting font from a computer, clip art alphabet book, or by drawing the letters freehand. Use three strands of embroidery floss and satin stitch. After fabric is embroidered, trim to 4" x 6". Turn raw edges under ¼" on all sides and press.

4. Fold unit from step 2 in half lengthwise to find center. Unfold and position monogrammed piece from step 3 on Fabric B strip as shown. Edge stitch in place.

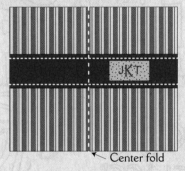

JKT

← Center fold

5. Turn top edge of laundry bag under ¼" and press.

6. Fold bag in half lengthwise with right sides together and side and bottom raw edges aligned. Beginning at top, sew 1¾" down side of bag. Backstitch. Leave 1" opening, backstitch, then continue sewing side and bottom seams as shown. Reinforce seam by stitching a parallel row ⅛" from first row as shown.

1¾
Leave open 1"

fold line

wrong side

7. Fold and pin top edge 1½" to wrong side of bag. Edge stitch close to hem and stitch again ⅛" from previous stitching as shown.

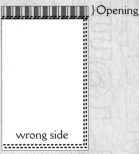

}Opening

wrong side

8. Turn bag to right side. Use safety pin to insert cording through side seam opening. Add cord lock and knot ends of cording.

A wedding is a joy-filled occasion,...

...the start of a **new life together**. Express your **glad-hearted greetings** for newlyweds or a couple celebrating an anniversary with a colorful quilt featuring over-sized blocks and **twining flowers** and vines.

Complement the quilt with a wallhanging and gathering of pillows for a decorator touch.

This beautiful quilt will be a **treasured keepsake** for the happy couple and a **loving reminder** of that special day and their **first home together**.

Sweethearts Bed Quilt

Joyful memories will be woven into every stitch of this special quilt. A single flower at the heart of the appliqué motif symbolizes a joyous union while vines, berries, and flowers represent the blooming and growth of a new family. Pieced blocks provide a framework and support for the flowering appliqués. Beautiful and functional, this large quilt is the perfect wedding or anniversary gift and will be a delightful addition to any bedroom. This quilt is sure to become a family heirloom preserving memories of a joy-filled day for generations to come.

Sweetheart Bed Quilt 97" x 97"	FIRST CUT		SECOND CUT	
	Number of Strips or Pieces	Dimensions	Number of Pieces	Dimensions
Fabric A Background & Border Pieces 7⅓ yards	4	21" squares		
	38	4½" x 42	304	4½" squares
Fabric B Center Block Pieces ½ yard	3	4½" x 42"	18	4½" squares
Fabric C Center Block Pieces & Appliqué Accent Strips 1⅙ yards	3	4½" x 42"	18	4½" squares
	16	1½" x 42"	8	1½" x 23"
			8	1½" x 21"
Fabric D Block Pieces 1¼ yards	9	4½" x 42"	36	4½" x 8½"
Fabric E Block Pieces 2 yards	14	4½" x 42"	36	4½" x 8½"
			36	4½" squares
Fabric F Block Pieces & Border Pieces 2¾ yards	4	7" x 42"	18	7" squares (cut twice diagonally to make 72 Small Triangles)
	2	6⅝" x 42"	12	6⅝" squares (cut once diagonally to make 24 Large Triangles)
	11	4½" x 42"	44	4½" x 8½" (Border)
Fabric G Side & Corner Setting Triangles 1½ yards	2	25¼" squares (cut twice diagonally to make Side Setting Triangle)		
	2	8⅞" squares (cut once diagonally to make Corner Triangles)		
Binding ¼ yard ¾ yard	2	2¾" x 42" (Dark Corner Binding)		
	9	2¾" x 42" (Light Side Binding)		

Backing - 8¾ yards
Batting - 105" x 105"
Berry Appliqués - Scraps
Small Flower Appliqués - ¼ yard
Large Flower Appliqués - ¼ yard
Leaf & Stems Appliqués - ½ yard
Flower Center Appliqués - Assorted Scraps
Lightweight Fusible Web - 5 yards

Fabric Requirements and Cutting Instructions

Read all instructions before beginning and use ¼"-wide seam allowances throughout. Read Cutting Strips and Pieces on page 92 prior to cutting fabric.

Getting Started

This quilt is made of two different 23" squares (unfinished) set on point; nine pieced blocks; and four appliqué blocks. The pieced blocks go together quickly using the Quick Corner Triangle method. The appliqué blocks are made using Quick-Fuse Appliqué and then finished with decorative machine stitching. The blocks are set on point, with side-and corner-setting triangles. A Flying Geese border (eleven "geese" per side) frames the quilt.

Refer to Accurate Seam Allowance on page 92. Whenever possible, use the Assembly Line Method on page 92. Press seams in direction of arrows.

Pieced Blocks

1. Refer to Quick Corner Triangles on page 92. Make a quick corner triangle using one 4½" Fabric A square and one 4½" Fabric C square as shown. Press. Make eighteen. Make quick corner triangles using one 4½" Fabric A square and one 4½" Fabric B square as shown. Press. Make eighteen.

A = 4½ x 4½
C = 4½ x 4½
Make 18

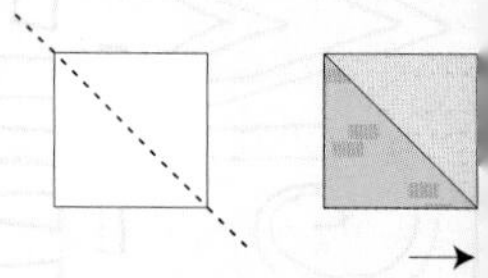

A = 4½ x 4½
B = 4½ x 4½
Make 18

2. Sew two units (one of each combination) from step 1 together in pairs as shown. Press. Make eighteen. Sew together in pairs as shown. Press. Make nine.

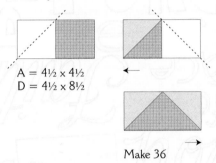

Make 18

Make 9

3. Making quick corner triangle units, sew two 4½" Fabric A squares to one 4½" x 8½" Fabric D piece as shown. Press. Make thirty-six.

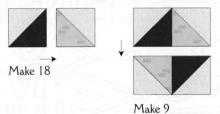

A = 4½ x 4½
D = 4½ x 8½

Make 36

4. Making quick corner triangle units, sew two 4½" Fabric A squares to one 4½" x 8½" Fabric E piece as shown. Press. Make thirty-six.

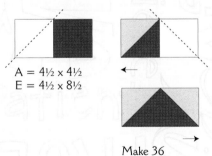

A = 4½ x 4½
E = 4½ x 8½

Make 36

5. Arrange and sew together two units from step 4, two units from step 3, and one unit from step 2 as shown. Press. Make nine.

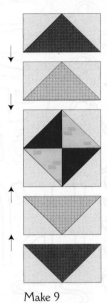

Make 9

6. Making a quick corner triangle unit, sew one 4½" Fabric A square to one 4½" Fabric E square as shown. Press. Make thirty-six.

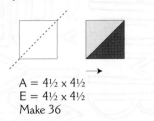

A = 4½ x 4½
E = 4½ x 4½
Make 36

Sweethearts Bed Quilt
Finished Size: 97" x 97"

7. Sew one unit from step 3 between two units from step 6 as shown. Press. Make eighteen.

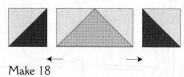

Make 18

8. Sew one unit from step 7 between two Small Fabric F Triangles as shown. Press. Make eighteen.

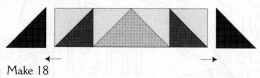

Make 18

9. Sew one unit from step 4 between two Small Fabric F Triangles as shown. Press. Make eighteen.

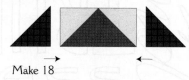

Make 18

10. Sew one unit from step 8 to one unit from step 9 as shown. Press. Make eighteen.

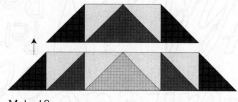

Make 18

11. Sew one unit from step 5 between two units from step 10 as shown. Press. Make nine. Block measures 24½" x 24½" at longest points.

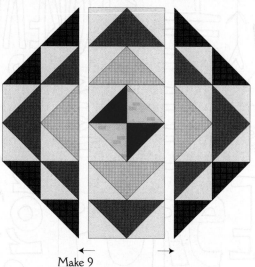

Make 9
Block measures 24½" x 24½"

Appliqué Blocks

Refer to appliqué instructions on page 93. Our instructions are for Quick-Fuse Appliqué, but if you prefer hand appliqué, reverse templates and add ¼"-wide seam allowance.

1. Use patterns on pages 46 and 47 to trace four large flowers, sixteen small flowers, sixteen stems, sixteen berries, sixteen large leaves, and thirty-two small leaves. Use appropriate fabrics to prepare all appliqués for fusing.

2. Refer to photo on page 40 and layout to position and fuse appliqués on one 21" Fabric A square. Finish appliqués with machine satin stitch or other decorative stitching as desired. Press. Make four.

3. Sew one unit from step 2 between two 1½" x 21" Fabric C strips. Press seams toward strips. Sew 1½" x 23" Fabric C strips to sides. Press. Make four. Block measures 23" square.

Assembly

Quilt is assembled in diagonal rows. Arrange pieced and appliqué blocks, Large Fabric F Triangles, Fabric G Side-Setting Triangles, and Fabric G Corner-Setting Triangles in diagonal rows as shown. Sew Fabric F triangles to Pieced Blocks. Press. Sew together blocks and Side-Setting Triangles to make diagonal rows. Press seams in opposite directions from row to row. Sew Corner-Setting Triangles to quilt. Press. Sew diagonal rows together. Press.

Borders

1. Making quick corner triangle units, sew two 4½" Fabric A squares to one 4½" x 8½" Fabric F piece as shown. Press. Make forty-four.

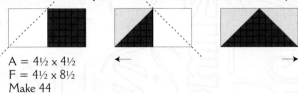

A = 4½ x 4½
F = 4½ x 8½
Make 44

2. Arrange and sew together eleven units from step 1. Press. Make four.

Make 4

3. Remove two end triangles from border strips from step 2 as shown. Make four.

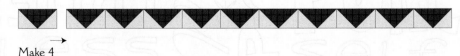

remove   Make 4   remove

4. Sew border strips from step 3 to top, bottom, and sides of quilt. Press seams toward quilt top.

Layering and Finishing

1. Cut backing crosswise into three equal pieces. Sew pieces together to make one 105" x 120" (approximate) backing piece. Press and trim to 105" x 105".

2. Arrange and baste backing, batting, and top together, referring to Layering the Quilt on page 94. Hand or machine quilt as desired.

3. Refer to Binding the Quilt on page 95. Cut four 2¾" x 13" blue binding pieces. Referring to photo on page 40 and layout, sew blue binding to quilt corners. Binding should extend ½" on both sides of quilt past edge. Sew 2¾" x 42" ivory binding strips end-to-end to make one continuous 2¾"-wide strip. Cut four 2¾" x 82" ivory binding pieces and sew to top, bottom and sides of quilt, including binding just added. Turn side binding to back of quilt first, trimming as necessary, then top and bottom. Turn corner binding last folding under ¼" raw edge. Hand-stitch in place.

Memories

New Business Bliss

I officially launched my pattern business at Quilt Market in Houston, Texas with the name "Mumm's the Word." This is my original h a n d - d r a w n logo. Naturally, I really had no idea if anyone would like my patterns or not. But they did like them, and they came to my booth, and ordered patterns for their stores. After I returned home, the orders kept coming in. Then I realized that I had to fill them!

In no time, I also realized I needed help! I hired teenagers to help me fold, glue on photos and pack patterns. They worked on my dining room table, then out of my guest room and soon after out of my basement that I turned into a mini shipping office. This all worked pretty well as long as I picked the teens up after school and dropped them off at their homes after work!

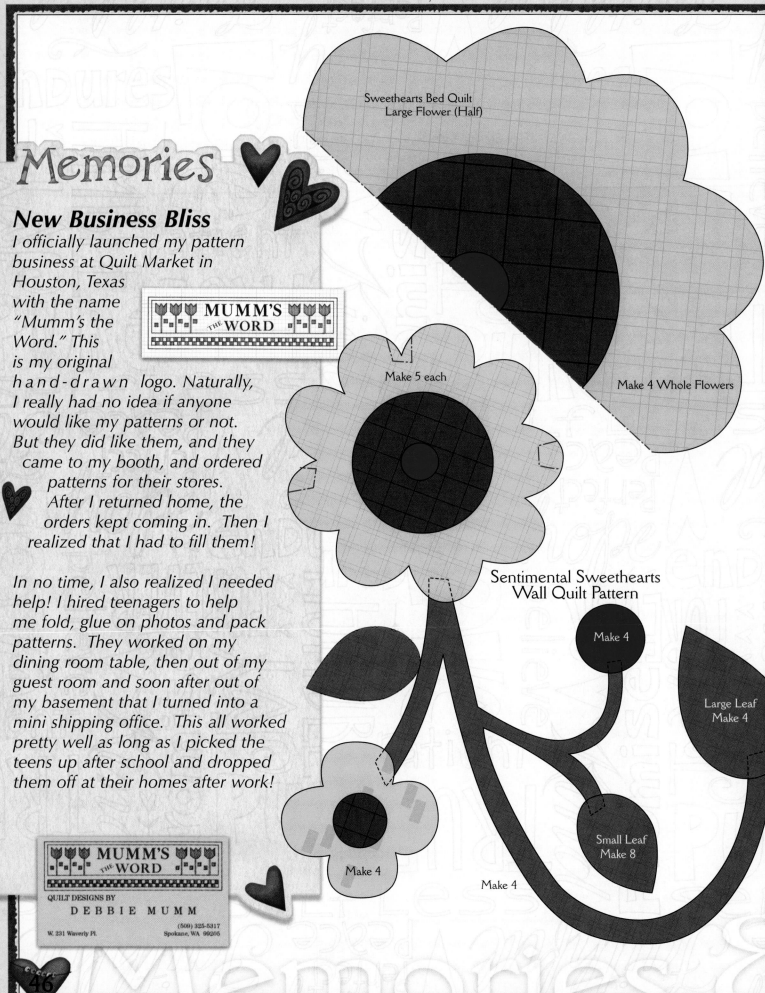

Sweethearts Bed Quilt
Large Flower (Half)

Make 4 Whole Flowers

Make 5 each

Sentimental Sweethearts
Wall Quilt Pattern

Make 4

Large Leaf
Make 4

Small Leaf
Make 8

Make 4

Make 4

MUMM'S THE WORD

QUILT DESIGNS BY
DEBBIE MUMM
W. 231 Waverly Pl.   (509) 325-5317
                            Spokane, WA 99205

46

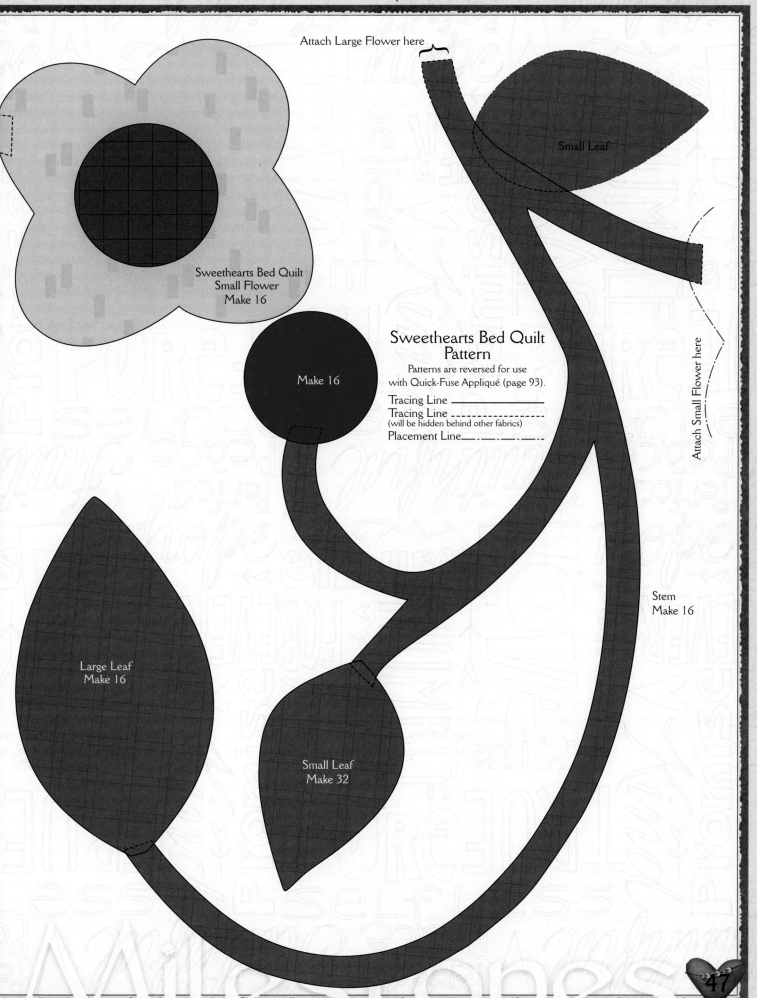

Attach Large Flower here

Small Leaf

Sweethearts Bed Quilt
Small Flower
Make 16

Make 16

Attach Small Flower here

Sweethearts Bed Quilt Pattern

Patterns are reversed for use
with Quick-Fuse Appliqué (page 93).

Tracing Line _____
Tracing Line ------------------
(will be hidden behind other fabrics)
Placement Line ___.___.___.___.

Stem
Make 16

Large Leaf
Make 16

Small Leaf
Make 32

Sentimental Sweethearts Wall Quilt

Celebrate a wedding or milestone anniversary or "just because" with this beautiful wall quilt. Used by itself or to complement the Sweethearts Bed Quilt, this medallion-style quilt will say "I love you" in every stitch. If desired, embroidery can be added to permanently commemorate a joyful occasion. Sweet memories of one of life's milestone moments will be forever prompted by this sentimental quilt.

Sentimental Sweethearts Wall Quilt 45" x 45"	FIRST CUT		SECOND CUT	
	Number of Strips or Pieces	Dimensions	Number of Pieces	Dimensions
Fabric A Background & Pieced Border 1 yard	1	10½" x 42"	1	10½" square
			4	8½" x 2½"*
	4	4½" x 42"	28	4½" squares
	2	2½" x 42	24	2½" squares
Fabric B Block Pieces ⅓ yard	3	2½" x 42"	40	2½" squares
Fabric C Corner Squares, Leaf & Stem Appliqués ¼ yard	4	2½" squares		
Fabric D Corner Squares ⅛ yard	4	2½" squares		
Fabric E Pieced Border ⅝ yard	3	4½" x 42"	20	4½" squares
	2	2½" x 42"	8	2½" x 5½"
Fabric F Pieced Border ½ yard	3	4½" x 42"	20	4½" squares

*Sizes to be cut for piecing after embroidering if desired.

Sentimental Sweethearts Wall Quilt continued	FIRST CUT		SECOND CUT	
	Number of Strips or Pieces	Dimensions	Number of Pieces	Dimensions
Fabric G Appliqué Accent Border & Pieced Border ½ yard	3	4½" x 42"	24	4½" squares
	2	1" x 42"	2	1" x 11½"
			2	1" x 10½"
BORDERS				
First Border ⅛ yard	2	1½" x 42"	2	1½" x 18½"
			2	1½" x 16½"
Second Border & Third Border ⅜ yard	8	1½" x 42"	4	1½" x 32½"
			2	1½" x 24½"
			2	1½" x 22½"
Fourth Border ¼ yard	4	1½" x 42"	4	1½" x 32½"
Outside Border ¾ yard	5	4½" x 42"	2	2½" x 36½"
Binding ½ yard	5	2¾" x 42"		

Backing - 2¾ yards
Batting - 49" x 49"
Five Large Flower Appliqués - ⅛ yard
Four Small Flower Appliqués - Assorted Scraps
Berry Appliqués - Assorted Scraps
Lightweight Fusible Web - 1 yard

Fabric Requirements and Cutting Instructions

Read all instructions before beginning and use ¼"-wide seam allowances throughout. Read Cutting Strips and Pieces on page 92 prior to cutting fabric.

Getting Started

This medallion-style quilt consists of a center appliqué block, fused and finished with machine stitching. The center block is set on point with over-sized setting triangles consisting of quick corner triangle units. The Embroidery Border has four 8½" x 2½" pieces that can be personalized with a celebration message with either hand or machine embroidery. The Triangle Pieced Border consists of quick corner triangles. Pay extra attention to the placement of units before sewing to ensure correct triangle positions.

Refer to Accurate Seam allowance on page 92. Whenever possible, use the Assembly Line Method on page 92. Press seams in directions of arrows.

Adding the Appliqués

Refer to appliqué instructions on page 93. Our instructions are for Quick-Fuse Appliqué, but if you prefer hand applique, add ¼"-wide seam allowances.

1. Use pattern on page 46 to trace five large flowers, four small flowers, four stems, four berries, four large leaves, and eight small leaves. Use assorted scraps to prepare all appliqués for fusing.

2. Refer to photo on page 48 and layout to position and fuse appliqués to 10½" Fabric A square and a large flower to four 4½" Fabric A squares. Finish appliqué edges with machine satin stitch or other decorative stitching as desired.

3. Sew 1" x 10½" Fabric G strip to top and bottom of 10½" applique square. Press seams toward strips. Sew 1" x 11½" Fabric G strips to sides. Press.

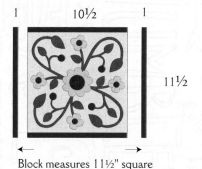

Block measures 11½" square

Sentimental Sweethearts Wall Quilt
Finished Size: 45" x 45"

Pieced Triangle Units

1. Refer to Quick Corner Triangles on page 92. Making a quick corner triangle unit, sew one 2½" Fabric A square to one 2½" Fabric B square as shown. Press. Make twenty-four.

A = 2½ x 2½
B = 2½ x 2½
Make 24

2. Sew three units from step 1 together as shown. Press. Make four. Sew two units from step 1 together as shown. Press. Make four.

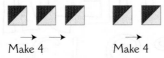

Make 4   Make 4

3. Sew one 2½" Fabric B square to the side of each unit in step 2 as shown. Press. Make four of each. Sew 2½" Fabric B squares to the side and bottom of each remaining unit from step 1 as shown. Press. Make four.

2½

2½

Make 4

2½

2½

Make 4

2½ 2½

2½

2½

Make 4

4. Arrange and sew the three units from step 3 as shown. Press. Make four.

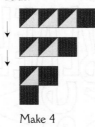

Make 4

5. Using a see-through ruler, align the ¼" mark at the center of Fabric B squares as shown. Trim.

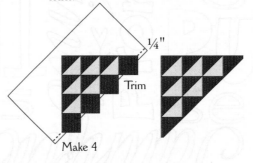

¼"

Trim

Make 4

Center Medallion

1. Sew pieced triangle units to opposite sides of the medallion appliqué as shown. Triangles will extend beyond raw edges of squares. Press seams toward Accent Border. Sew pieced triangles to remaining sides. Press. Block measures 16½" square.

Block measures 16½" square

Borders

1. Arrange and sew 1½" x 16½" First Border strips to top and bottom of Center Medallion. Press seams toward border. Sew 1½" x 18½" First Border strips to sides. Press.

2. If desired, machine or hand embroider message on Fabric A pieces before cutting to 8½" x 2½". Sew one 8½" x 2½" Fabric A piece between two 2½" x 5½" Fabric E pieces. Press. Make four.

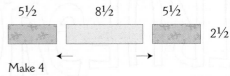

5½   8½   5½

2½

Make 4

3. Sew unit from step 1 between two units from step 2. Press seams toward First Border.

4. Sew one unit from step 2 between two 2½" Fabric C squares. Press. Make two. Sew these units to sides of unit from step 3.

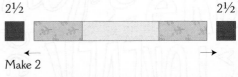

2½   2½

Make 2

5. Arrange and sew 1½" x 22½" Second Border strips to top and bottom of unit from step 4. Press seams toward Second Border. Sew 1½" x 24½" Second Border strips to sides. Press.

Triangle Pieced Border

1. Refer to Quick Corner Triangles on page 92. Making a quick corner triangle unit, sew one 4½" Fabric A square to one 4½" Fabric F square as shown. Press. Make twenty and label Block 1. Making a quick corner triangle unit, sew one 4½" Fabric G square to one 4½" Fabric E square as shown. Press. Make sixteen and label Block 2.

Block 1   **Block 2**

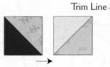

A = 4½ x 4½   G = 4½ x 4½
F = 4½ x 4½   E = 4½ x 4½
Make 20   Make 16

2. Making a quick corner triangle unit, sew one Block 1 to one Block 2 as shown. Blocks must be placed in exact position as shown to have correct placement of triangles. Press. Make sixteen.

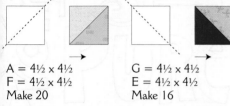

Trim Line

Place on top of Block 1   Make 16

3. Making a quick corner triangle unit, sew one 4½" Fabric G square to Block 1 from step 1. Press. Make four.

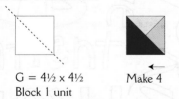

G = 4½ x 4½   Make 4
Block 1 unit

4. Making a quick corner triangle unit, sew one 4½" Fabric A square to one 4½" Fabric E square. Press. Make four.

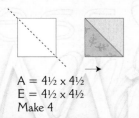

A = 4½ x 4½
E = 4½ x 4½
Make 4

5. Making a quick corner triangle unit, sew one 4½" Fabric G square to one unit from step 4. Press. Make four.

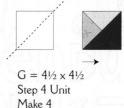

G = 4½ x 4½
Step 4 Unit
Make 4

6. Arrange and sew together one unit from step 3, four units from step 2, and one unit from step 5 as shown. Press. Make four.

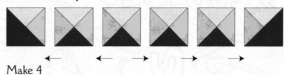

Make 4

7. Referring to photo on page 48 and layout on page 49, sew Center Medallion between two units from step 6. Press seams toward Second Border.

8. Sew one unit from step 6 between two 4½" Fabric A appliquéd squares. Press seams toward Fabric A. Make two. Sew these units to sides of Center Medallion unit.

Finishing Borders

1. Sew one 1½" x 32½" Fourth Border strip lengthwise to one 1½" x 32½" Third Border strip. Press. Make four.

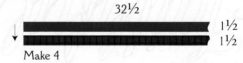

32½

1½
1½

Make 4

2. Referring to photo and layout on page 49, arrange and sew one unit from step 1 to top and bottom of the quilt. Press seams toward border strips. Sew one 2½" Fabric D square to each end of two remaining strips from step 1. Press. Sew this unit to sides. Press.

3. Sew 4½" x 36½" Outside Border strips to top and bottom of quilt. Press seams toward border. Piece and trim remaining Outside Border strips to measure 4½" x 44½". Make two. Sew to sides of quilt.

Layering & Finishing

1. Cut backing crosswise into two equal pieces. Sew pieces together to make one 49" x 80" (approximate) backing piece. Press and trim to 49" x 49".

2. Arrange and baste backing, batting, and top together, referring to Layering the Quilt on page 94.

3. Machine or hand quilt as desired.

4. Sew 2¾" x 42" binding strips end-to-end to make one continuous 2¾"-wide strip. Refer to Binding the Quilt on page 95 and bind the quilt.

Friends influence us forever...

...It's hard to pinpoint the moment a friendship begins, but those lifetime friendships can be among the most **influential relationships** in our lives.

Celebrate the sharing of **soul-searching conversations** over many cups of coffee with this unique gift for a **special friend**.
Fabrics are layered one on top of the other to represent the many layers of a deep friendship.

Topsy-turvy cups and pots are embellished with beads, buttons, and rickrack to remind you of the **fun and laughs** shared over the years.

Coffee & Conversation Wall Quilt

What better way to salute a long-lasting friendship and hundreds of fun memories than with tea or coffee and conversation! Celebrate the many facets of friendship with a multi-layered memento featuring a wide variety of playful cups and pots. Get together and make two so you can each have one, or make one to send to a faraway friend just to let her know that you are thinking of her.

Coffee & Conversation Wall Quilt 25" x 32"	FIRST CUT	
	Number of Strips or Pieces	Dimensions
BLOCKS & BACKGROUND APPLIQUÉS		
Fabric A ¼ yard	2	6½" squares
Fabric B & Binding ⅝ yard	1	6½" square
	1	5½" square
	1	4½" square
	4	2¾" x 42" (Binding)
Fabric C ¼ yard	2	7½" squares
Fabric D ¼ yard	1	6½" square
	1	4½" x 6½"
	1	1½" x 6½"
Fabric E ⅓ yard	1	8½" x 9½"
	1	4½" square
Fabric F ¼ yard	1	7½" x 6½"
Fabric G ¼ yard	1	6½" square
	1	5½" x 4½"
Fabric H ¼ yard	1	6½" x 7½"
	1	6½" square
	2	1½" x 6½"
Fabric I ¼ yard	1	4½" square
	1	1½" x 7½"
	1	1½" x 6½"
Fabric J ¼ yard	1	6½" x 7½"
	1	4½" square
Fabric K ⅙ yard	1	4½" x 5½"
	1	4½" square
Fabric L ⅛ yard	1	1½" x 7½"
	1	1½" x 4½"
Fabric M ⅙ yard	1	4½" square
	1	1½" x 4½"
Fabric N ⅙ yard	1	4½" x 2½"
BORDERS		
First Border ⅙ yard	2	1" x 20½"
	2	1" x 28½"
Outside Border & Background ½ yard	2	2" x 21½"
	2	2" x 31½"
	1	5½" square

Backing - 1 yard
Batting - 29" x 36"
Lightweight Fusible Web - ½ yard
Assorted Coffee Pot & Cup Appliqués - Assorted scraps
Embellishments - Small buttons, beads, seed beads, & assorted rickrack

Fabric Requirements and Cutting Instructions

Read all instructions before beginning and use ¼"-wide seam allowances throughout. Read Cutting Strips and Pieces on page 92 prior to cutting fabric.

Getting Started

This quilt includes twelve appliqué blocks in varying sizes, featuring embellishments such as beads, buttons, and rickrack. Each block is fused and appliquéd to the block square. The rickrack details are sewn before the blocks are assembled. Beads and buttons are added after quilting.

Extra yardage is given for the blocks and appliqué backgrounds so there are ample scraps to make the coffee pots, cups, and sashing strips. Use a variety of assorted scraps for small appliqué details, such as cup handles, saucers, and coffee pot lids.

Making the Blocks

Refer to appliqué instructions on page 93. Our instructions are for Quick-Fuse Appliqué. If you prefer hand appliqué, reverse templates and add ¼"-wide seam allowances.

1. Use patterns on pages 60 and 61 to trace all coffee pot and cup appliqués on paper side of fusible web. Use assorted scraps to prepare one of each piece for fusing. Since there are many small pieces, place prepared appliqués in labeled envelopes.

2. Refer to photo and block layout on page 52 to position and fuse Cup 1 appliqués on 4½" Fabric I square. Position and pin appliquéd block on one 6½" Fabric A square slightly askew as shown. Use a machine zigzag stitch to attach Fabric I. Finish appliqués with machine

satin stitch or decorative stitching as desired. Trim a piece of wide rickrack as shown and machine or hand stitch above cup for "steam."

Block 1

6½

6½

3. Repeat step 2 using Coffee Cup 2 and fuse appliqués on 4½" Fabric K square. Stitch appliquéd square to 6½" Fabric B square as shown. Finish appliqués with decorative stitching. Machine or hand stitch two rows of small rickrack to top and bottom of cup as shown. Sew 1½" x 6½" Fabric H piece to right side of block. Press.

Block 2

6½ 1½

6½

4. Repeat process using Coffee Pot 3 and fuse on 5½" Outside Border fabric square. Stitch appliquéd square to one 7½" Fabric C square as shown. Finish appliqués with decorative stitching.

Block 3

7½

7½

5. Repeat process using Coffee Cup 4 and fuse on 4½" x 2½" Fabric N piece. Stitch appliquéd piece to 4½" x 6½" Fabric D piece as shown. Finish appliqués with decorative stitching. Sew block between 1½" x 4½" Fabric L and 1½" x 4½" Fabric M pieces. Press.

Block 4

4½

1½

6½

1½

6. Repeat process using Coffee Pot 5 and fuse on 6½" x 7½" Fabric H piece. Stitch appliquéd piece to 8½" x 9½" Fabric E piece as shown. Arrange and sew rickrack onto pot. Finish appliqués with decorative stitching. Trim a wide rickrack piece as shown and machine or hand stitch above spout for "steam."

Block 5

9½

8½

7. Repeat process using Coffee Cup 6 and fuse on 5½" x 4½" Fabric G piece. Stitch appliquéd piece to 7½" x 6½" Fabric F piece as shown. Finish appliqués with decorative stitching. Machine or hand stitch wide piece of rickrack across cup as shown. Sew 1½" x 7½" Fabric I piece to top of block. Press.

Block 6

7½

1½

6½

Coffee & Conversation Wall Quilt
Finished Size: 25" x 32"

8. Repeat process using Coffee Cup 7 and fuse onto 4½" Fabric J square. Stitch appliquéd square to 6½" Fabric G square as shown. Finish appliqués with decorative stitching. Machine or hand stitch two pieces of narrow rickrack above cup as shown. Sew one 1½" x 6½" Fabric I piece to right side of block. Press.

Block 7

6½   1½

6½

9. Repeat process using Coffee Cup 8 and fuse on 4½" Fabric M square. Stitch appliquéd piece to 6½" Fabric A square as shown. Finish appliqués with decorative stitching.

Block 8

6½

6½

10. Repeat process using Coffee Cup 9 and fuse appliqués onto 4½" Fabric B square. Stitch appliquéd square to 6½" Fabric D square as shown. Finish appliqués with decorative stitching. Machine or hand stitch two pieces of narrow rickrack above cup as shown. Sew 1½" x 6½" Fabric H piece to right side of block. Press.

Block 9

6½   1½

6½

11. Repeat process using Coffee Pot 10 and fuse on 5½" Fabric B square. Stitch appliquéd square to 7½" Fabric C square as shown. Finish appliqués with decorative stitching.

Block 10

7½

7½

12. Repeat process using Coffee Cup 11 and fuse on 4½" Fabric E square. Stitch appliquéd square to 6½" Fabric H square as shown. Finish appliqués with decorative stitching. Sew 1½" x 6½" Fabric D piece to bottom of block. Press.

Block 11

6½

6½

1½

13. Repeat process using Coffee Cup 12 and fuse onto 4½" x 5½" Fabric K piece. Stitch appliquéd piece to 6½" x 7½" Fabric J piece as shown. Finish appliqués with decorative stitching. Machine or hand stitch a piece of wide rickrack above cup as shown. Sew 1½" x 7½" Fabric L piece to left side of block. Press.

Block 12

1½   6½

7½

Assembly

1. Arrange and sew Blocks 1 and 2 together as shown. Press. Arrange and sew Block 4 and Block 5 together. Press. Sew block pairs together. Press.

2. Arrange and sew Block 3 to the top of Block 6 as shown. Press. Sew the block pair to the right side of unit from step 1. Press.

3. Sew Block 8 between Blocks 7 and Block 9 as shown. Press. Sew Block 11 between Block 10 and Block 12. Press. Sew the two block sets together. Press.

4. Refer to photo on page 52 and layout on page 55. Sew unit from step 2 to top of unit from step 3. Press.

Borders

1. Sew 1" x 20½" First Border strips to top and bottom of quilt. Press seams toward border.

2. Sew 1" x 28½" First Border strips to sides of quilt. Press.

3. Sew 2" x 21½" Outside Border strips to top and bottom of quilt. Press. Sew 2" x 31½" Outside Border strips to sides. Press.

Layering & Finishing

1. Trim backing fabric to measure approximately 29" x 36".

2. Arrange and baste backing, batting, and top together, referring to Layering the Quilt on page 94. Hand or machine quilt as desired.

3. Sew 2¾" x 42" binding strips end-to-end to make one continuous 2¾"-wide strip. Refer to Binding the Quilt on page 95 and bind to finish.

4. Refer to photo on page 52 and layout on page 55 to add decorative trims, buttons, and beads as desired.

Conversation Placemats

Finished Size: 16" x 12"
Each placemat features a coffee pot that is fused and appliquéd to a background square and then appliquéd to the placemat fabric.

Materials Needed

For four placemats

Fabric A - ¾ yard
  Four 10½" x 14½" pieces
Fabric B - ⅓ yard
  Four 8" squares
Fabric C - ¼ yard
  Four 6" squares
Border - ½ yard
  Eight 1½" x 14½" strips
  Eight 1½" x 12½" strips
Coffee Pot Appliqués - Scraps
Backing - ⅞ yard
  Four 13" x 17" pieces
Lightweight Batting -
  Four 13" x 17" pieces
Lightweight Fusible Web - ¼ yard

Making and Appliquéing the Placemats

Refer to appliqué instructions on page 93. Our instructions are for Quick-Fuse Appliqué, but if you prefer hand appliqué, reverse templates and add ¼"-wide seam allowances.

1. Sew 1½" x 14½" Border strip to top and bottom of one 14½" x 10½" Fabric A piece. Press seams toward border. Sew a 1½" x 12½" Border strip to sides as shown. Press. Make four.

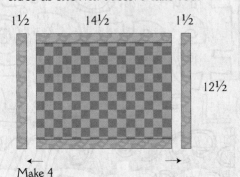

1½   14½   1½

12½

Make 4

2. Refer to Quick-Fuse Appliqué on page 93 and Coffee Pot patterns on page 60 and 61. Trace on paper side of fusible web one of each piece for two coffee pots, and two of each piece for one pot to make a total of four Coffee Pots. You may wish to reverse the fourth pot for a different look. Use assorted scraps to prepare appliqués for fusing.

3. Refer to photo to position and fuse each pot on one 6" Fabric C square. Finish appliqué edges with machine satin stitch or decorative stitching as desired. Position and pin appliquéd unit on one 8" Fabric B square and use a machine zigzag stitch to finish edges. Make four, varying slant of appliquéd block on each placemat.

4. Position and machine appliqué with a zigzag stitch, block from step 3 to center of each bordered placemat, once again varying slant of the blocks. Make four.

Layering and Finishing

1. Layer and center placemat top and backing right sides together on batting. Using a ¼"-wide seam, stitch around placemat edges, leaving a 4" opening on one long edge for turning. Trim batting close to stitching and backing even with placemat edges. Clip corners, turn, and press. Hand stitch opening closed.

2. Machine or hand quilt as desired. Add beads, buttons, and other embellishments as desired.

Coffee & Conversation Table Runner

Gather 'round the kitchen table for some lively conversation and your favorite beverage! This table runner is as spontaneous and fun as your conversations! Lots of playful patterns and lively layers are topped with quirky cups for a table runner that's also a conversation piece. Sharing memories and everyday doings makes the kitchen table the heart of the home!

Coffee & Conversation Table Runner 48" x 13½"	FIRST CUT		SECOND CUT	
	Number of Strips or Pieces	Dimensions	Number of Pieces	Dimensions
Fabric A Background Setting Triangles ½ yard	2	12⅝" squares (Cut twice diagonally to make 8 triangles)		
Fabric B Background Squares ⅓ yard each of two fabrics	2*	8½" squares *cut for each fabric		
Border ⅙ yard	4	1" x 42"	2 2	1" x 9¼" 1" x 8¾"
Binding ⅜ yard	4	2¾" x 42"		

First Layer Squares - Assorted scraps - one 4½" square from four different fabrics
Second Layer Squares - Assorted scraps - one 6" square from four different fabrics
Cup Appliqués - Assorted scraps
Backing - ⅞ yard
Batting - 18" x 52"
Lightweight Fusible Web - ¼ yard
Embroidery Floss - Yellow, tan, orange, green
Embellishments - Assorted Rickrack, Five Star Buttons
Tassels, Two Large Beads, Two Small Beads

Fabric Requirements and Cutting Instructions

Read all instructions before beginning and use ¼"-wide seam allowances throughout. Read Cutting Strips and Pieces on page 92 prior to cutting fabric.

Getting Started

This table runner features four scrappy, appliquéd coffee cups that are quick-fused and stitched to 4½" scrappy squares. Rickrack embellishments are added as desired, and the squares are then tilted and layered on 6" and 8½" squares, and finished with decorative stitching. Buttons and tassels are added after quilting.

Refer to Accurate Seam Allowance on page 92. Whenever possible, use the Assembly Line Method on page 92. Press seams in direction of arrows.

Making the Table Runner

1. Arrange and sew Fabric A Setting Triangles to sides of 8½" Fabric B squares as shown. Press seams in opposite directions from row to row. Sew rows together. Press.

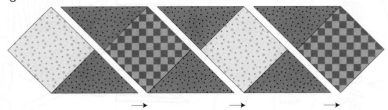

2. Sew 1" x 8¾" border strips to opposite sides of table runner corners as shown. Press seams toward borders. Sew 1" x 9¼" border strips to remaining corners, including border just added. Press. Trim border edges even with setting triangles.

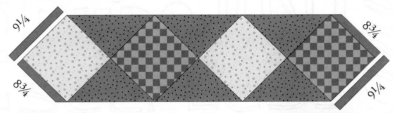

3. Sew remaining Border strips together end-to-end. Press. Cut in half crosswise and sew to long sides of table runner. Using a see-through ruler and rotary cutter, trim side border edges even with corners as shown.

Appliquéing the Table Runner

Refer to appliqué instructions on page 93. Our instructions are for Quick-Fuse Appliqué. If you prefer hand appliqué, reverse templates and add ¼"-wide seam allowances.

1. Refer to Quick-Fuse Appliqué on page 93. Use patterns on pages 60-61 to trace Coffee Cups 2, 7, 9, and 11 on paper side of fusible web. Use assorted scraps to prepare appliqués for fusing.

2. Refer to photo and block layouts to position and fuse each coffee cup on one scrappy 4½" fabric square. Finish appliqués with machine satin stitch or decorative stitching as desired. Machine or hand stitch rickrack embellishments to units as desired.

3. Position and pin each appliquéd block on one scrappy 6" square as shown. Use a machine zigzag stitch to attach edges of 4½" square.

4. Referring to photo, position and pin each appliquéd square from step 3 on table runner slanting blocks as shown. Secure appliquéd squares with a zigzag stitch.

Layering and Finishing

1. Cut backing fabric into two 18" x 27" pieces. With right sides together, sew pieces along one short end. Press.

2. Arrange and baste backing, batting, and table runner top together, referring to Layering the Quilt on page 94. Machine or hand quilt as desired.

3. Cut two 2¾" x 10½" and two 2¾" x 9¼" Binding pieces. Refer to Binding the Quilt on page 95 and Making the Table Runner, step 2. Sew 9¼"-long binding strips to opposite corners of table runner, press and trim. Referring to diagram, sew 10½"-long binding strips to remaining corners including binding just sewn. Trim binding edges even with sides.

4. Sew remaining binding pieces end-to-end to make one 2¾"-wide binding strip. Cut into two equal pieces. Sew binding strips to sides of table runner.

5. Press binding to back. Fold corners first then sides, turning raw edge under. Pin in position and hand stitch in place.

6. Referring to photo embellish as desired and add tassels on ends of table runner.

Coffee & Coversation Quilt Patterns

Patterns are reversed for use with Quick-Fuse Appliqué (page 93).

Tracing Line _____

Tracing Line ------------------
(will be hidden behind other fabrics)

Embellishment Placement
Line ----------------------

*Milestones

You Gotta Have Friends!

My first big break came in 1990 when a publisher approached me, said that she'd seen my patterns, she thought my directions were thorough and easy-to-understand, and asked if I was interested in doing a quilt book. I was so flattered and so excited about this opportunity, and what an opportunity it turned out to be!

I got the chance to work with real professionals from whom I learned so much. They produced a beautiful 256 page hardcover book of my designs, and they mailed out millions of direct mail pieces promoting my book.

Luckily the book sold very well and my name and credibility were now established. I ended up doing four more books with this publisher, Rodale Press.

The most significant turning points...

...in life can be the result of a **challenge**, hardship or illness. When someone is in the center of it all, that is the time to offer **comfort and support**. Show him how much you care with the **gift** of a comforting flannel quilt.

This sweet quilt sews up easily for a quick response when the need for **special attention** arises.

Heart appliqués signify your **loving thoughts** to wrap your friend in need with tenderness during trying times.

Use these same **heart** appliqués to make handmade cards to express your **loving sentiments**.

Roy's Comfort Quilt

When the going gets tough, the tough get sewing. Find solace and unleash a fountain of memories by sewing a quilt for someone who needs comfort and caring. This flannel favorite is filled with warm wishes and will bring as much comfort to the sewer as to the receiver. When someone dear is sick or hurting, this quilt will remind him of your love.

Roy's Comfort Quilt 61" x 67"	FIRST CUT		SECOND CUT	
	Number of Strips or Pieces	Dimensions	Number of Pieces	Dimensions
Fabric A Sashing Checks ⅝ yard	1	4½" x 42"	4	4½" x 8½"
	2	3½" x 42"	8	3½" x 9½"
	2	2½" x 42"	4	2½" x 10½"
Fabric B Block 1 Red Borders ⅓ yard	3	3" x 42"	2	3" x 18"
			8	3" x 8½"
Fabric C Block 1 Blue Dots ⅙ yard	1	3½" x 42"	1	3½" x 18"
Fabric D Block 1 Blue Borders ½ yard	4	3½" x 42"	2	3½" x 20"
			8	3½" x 10½"
Fabric E Block 1 Red Center ⅙ yard	1	4½" x 42"	1	4½" x 20"
Fabric F Blue Triangles ⅓ yard* each of two fabrics	1*	10½" x 42" *cut for each fabric	2*	10½" squares
Fabric G Gold Triangles ⅓ yard* each of two fabrics	1*	10½" x 42" *cut for each fabric	2*	10½" squares
Fabric H Block 3 Background ⅙ yard* each of four fabrics	1*	4½" x 42" *cut for each fabric	4*	4½" x 7½"
Fabric I Block 3 Borders ½ yard	6	2½" x 42"	8	2½" x 18½"
			8	2½" x 8½"
BORDERS				
First Border ½ yard	6	2½" x 42"		
Outside Border ⅞ yard	6	4½" x 42"		
Binding ⅝ yard	7	2¾" x 42"		

Backing - 3¾ yards   Batting - 67" x 73"
Heart Appliqués - Assorted Red Scraps
Lightweight Fusible Web - ⅓ yard

Fabric Requirements and Cutting Instructions

Read all instructions before beginning and use ¼"-wide seam allowances throughout. Read Cutting Strips and Pieces on page 92 prior to cutting fabric.

Getting Started

Three 12½" x 18½" (unfinished) rectangular blocks provide a unique look for this easy and quick-to-make quilt. "Primitive" appliquéd hearts add a bit of whimsy. These blocks and the resulting quilt work well for a group project. All are designed to get the finished quilt to its recipient quickly.

Refer to Accurate Seam Allowance on page 92. Whenever possible, use the Assembly Line Method on page 92. Press seams in direction of arrows.

Block 1

Refer to appliqué instructions on page 93. Our instructions are for Quick-Fuse Appliqué, but if you prefer hand appliqué, reverse templates and add ¼"-wide seam allowance.

1. Sew 3½" x 18" Fabric C strip between two 3" x 18" Fabric B strips to make a strip set as shown. Press. Cut four 3½"-wide segments.

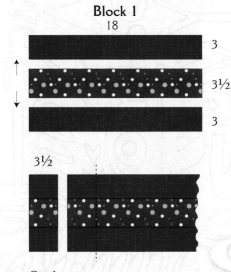

Block 1

Cut 4 segments

2. Sew together one 4½" x 8½" Fabric A piece, two 3" x 8½" Fabric B pieces, and one unit from step 1 as shown. Press. Make four.

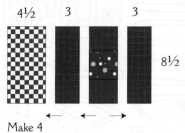

Make 4

3. Sew 4½" x 20" Fabric E strip between two 3½" x 20" Fabric D strips to make a strip set as shown. Press. Cut four 4½"-wide segments.

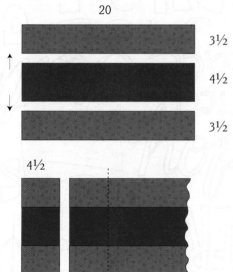

Cut 4 segments

4. Sew together two 3½" x 10½" Fabric D pieces, one unit from step 3, and one 2½" x 10½" Fabric A piece as shown. Press. Make four.

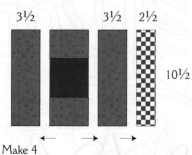

Make 4

5. Sew together units from step 2 and step 4 as shown. Press. Make four. Block measures 12½" x 18½".

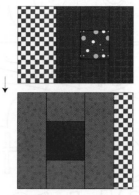

Make 4
Block measures 12½" x 18½"

6. Use pattern on page 68 to trace four Small Hearts onto paper side of fusible web. Use assorted scraps to prepare appliqués for fusing.

7. Refer to photo on page 62 and layout to position and fuse one small heart to each block as shown. Finish appliqué edges with machine blanket stitch or other decorative stitching as desired.

Block 1

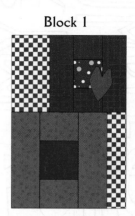

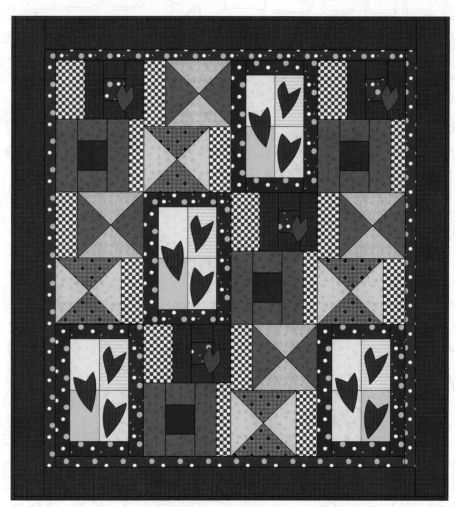

Roy's Comfort Quilt
Finished Size: 61" x 67"

Milestones

Beyond the Comfort Zone

One of the best things about making quilts is touching, buying, using, and collecting fabric! Back in the early ninties I was working on some new designs and really wanted some garden-themed fabric. I met with a fabric sales rep and asked her about garden-themed patterns. She didn't have what I was looking for and then said, "You should design some!" "Naw, I can't do that," was my response. "I'm too busy with my quilt pattern business." However, I just couldn't resist the idea, and within 24 hours of that conversation, I completed many of my first sketches for the line and that was the beginning of a new and immensely enjoyable venture.

Block 2

1. Draw diagonal line on wrong side of one 10½" Fabric G square. Place marked square and one 10½" Fabric F square right sides together. Sew scant ¼" away from drawn line on both sides to make half-square triangles as shown. Make four, two matching pairs of each combination. Cut on drawn line. Press. This will make eight half-square triangle units in matching sets of four.

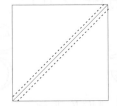
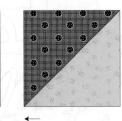

F = 10½ x 10½
G = 10½ x 10½
Make 4
(2 of each combination)

← Make 4   ← Make 4

2. Draw diagonal line on wrong side of one unit from step 1 in opposite direction from seam as shown. Place right sides together with unmarked matching unit from step 1, matching seam lines and placing Fabric G triangle on top of Fabric F triangle. Sew scant ¼" away from drawn line on both sides. Make four. Cut on drawn line. Press seams toward Fabric F, twisting center intersection (Tip on page 67). Square units to 9½". This will make eight quarter square-triangle units, four of each combination.

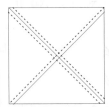
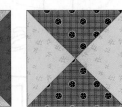

Units from step 16
Make 4
(2 of each combination)

Make 4
Square to 9½   Make 4
Square to 9½

3. Sew one 3½" x 9½" Fabric A piece to each unit from step 2 as shown. Make eight, four of each combination, noting orientation of triangles and position of Fabric A pieces as shown.

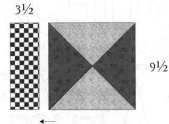

3½

9½

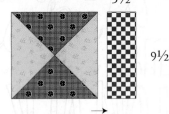

3½

9½

Make 8
(4 of each combination)

4. Sew units from step 3 together in pairs as shown. Press. Make four. Block 2 measures 12½" x 18½".

Block 2

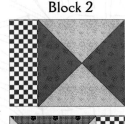

Make 4
Block measures 12½" x 18½"

1. Sew together two different 4½" x 7½" Fabric H pieces. Press. Make eight, four of each combination. Sew together one of each combination as shown. Press. Make four.

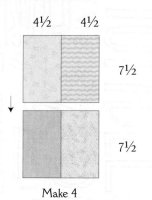

4½   4½

7½

7½

Make 4

2. Sew 2½" x 8½" Fabric I pieces to top and bottom of each unit from step 1 as shown. Press. Make four.

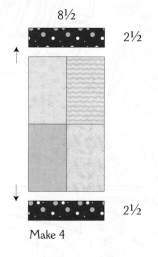

8½

2½

2½

Make 4

3. Sew 2½" x 18½" Fabric I pieces to sides of each unit from step 2 as shown. Press. Make four.

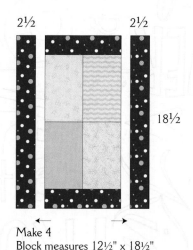

2½   2½

18½

Make 4
Block measures 12½" x 18½"

4. Refer to Quick-Fuse Appliqué on page 93 and use patterns on page 68 to trace Heart A and B on paper side of fusible web. Use assorted scraps to prepare four of Heart A and eight of Heart B.

5. Refer to photo on page 62 and layout on page 65 to position and fuse three hearts to each block. Finish appliqué edges with machine blanket stitch or other decorative stitching as desired.

Block 3

Make 4

Assembly

Refer to photo on page 62 and layout on page 65. Arrange and sew Blocks 1, 2, and 3 in three horizontal rows of four blocks each. Press seams in opposite directions from row to row. Sew rows together. Press.

Borders

1. Sew 2½" x 42" First Border strips together end-to-end to make one continuous 2½"-wide border strip. Press. Measure quilt through center from side to side. Cut two 2½"-wide First Border strips to this measurement. Sew to top and bottom of quilt. Press seams toward border.

2. Measure quilt through center from top to bottom including borders just added. Cut two 2½"-wide First Border strips to this measurement. Sew to sides of quilt. Press.

3. Refer to steps 1 and 2 to join, measure, trim, and sew 4½"-wide Outside Border strips to top, bottom, and sides of quilt. Press.

Layering and Finishing

1. Cut backing in half crosswise into two equal pieces. Sew pieces together lengthwise to make one 67" x 80" (approximate) backing piece. Press.

2. Arrange and baste backing, batting, and top together referring to Layering the Quilt on page 94. Hand or machine quilt as desired.

3. Sew 2¾" x 42" binding strips end-to-end to make one continuous 2¾"-wide binding strip. Refer to Binding the Quilt on page 95 and bind quilt to finish.

Tip for Twisting Seams

For ease in construction when using quarter-square triangles, we add a twist ...

When pressing the last seam, twist the center of the seam so that it fans into a square. Loosen stitches in the "square". Remove any stitches that prevent the square from laying flat. All seam allowances fan out in the same direction to eliminate excess bulk.

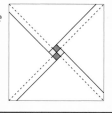

Memories

In Loving Remembrance

When you work with people over time, they become family. It's that way with our friends at South Sea Imports. Their sales manager, Roy Frym, was an important part of my business life for 10 years and when Roy got sick, we made a quilt hoping to bring him a little comfort. The Comfort Quilt is adapted from the quilt I designed for Roy and was made in loving remembrance of a special friendship.

Roy Frym
1935-2004

Heart Pattern A
Make 4

Heart Pattern B
Make 8

Small Heart Pattern
Make 8

Roy's Comfort Quilt
Heart Patterns
Patterns are reversed for use
with Quick-Fuse Appliqué (page 93).

Tracing Line _____

Handmade Cards

Say "thank you" or "thinking of you" with a handmade card. What better way to tell someone how much she means to you?

Materials Needed:

Fabric scraps in assorted colors and designs
Lightweight Fusible Web
Cardstock in assorted colors and textures
Decorative Papers in assorted prints and textures
Letter Stickers
Ink Pad
Scissors – small, sharp and pinking shears
Rotary Cutter
Scotch® Glue Stick Permanent Adhesive
Hot Glue Gun

Assembling the Cards:

Referring to photographs for design ideas, cut and layer cardstock and decorative papers in desired shapes and sizes. We used both paper and fabric for our motifs. Prepare fabric pieces following directions for Quick-Fuse Appliqué on page 93 and referring to Coffee Cup Pattern on page 61 or Large Heart Pattern. Fuse fabric pieces to cardstock or decorative papers using a medium-heat dry iron. Refer to Flower Pattern on page 77 and use cardstock for the Thank You Card flower. Decorate cards using techniques described below.

Weather/Antique Paper

This technique was used for the stem and leaves on the Thank You Card. Lightly mist cardstock pieces with water. Crumple, unfold, and re-crumple cardstock pieces until desired texture is achieved. Lay flat to dry. When cardstock pieces are dry, drag lightly over a black ink pad to highlight creases.

Add Decorative Brads

This technique was used on the Coffee Cup Card and Checked Thinking of You Card. Brads are available in many sizes, shapes, and colors for embellishing paper projects. Use a large needle to poke a hole for each brad, then insert a brad in each hole and open prongs.

Add Lettering

This technique is shown on all cards except the Coffee Cup Card. Using a computer, rubber stamps, hand lettering, or stickers (or any combination of these techniques) to add a sentiment to your card.

Add Buttons

This technique was used on the Thank You Card and Thinking of You Card. Using a needle and four strands of embroidery floss, attach buttons where desired, tying floss in a knot on the top side of button.

Add Other Embellishments

Rickrack, ribbons, and decorative trims can be adhered with glue. For the bead "steam" on the Coffee Cup Card, beads were sewn to the cardstock using needle and thread, placing four or five beads on each stitch.

So much to be grateful for...

...kindnesses and **considerations**, hospitality and generosity, **thoughtful caretaking**. Express your heartfelt thanks with an everlasting bouquet in the form of a **sweet**, little wall quilt.

These quilts may be small, but the message of **big thanks** will be perfectly conveyed. The **kindness of another** is something you carry with you always and your thank you gift will be treasured forever.

With three **delightful** designs from which to select, you'll find a quilt for any occasion. So, don't wait. Create a quilt to say **thank you**.

Many Thanks Quick Quilts

Express your gratitude with a lasting bouquet of flowers on a pert and pretty quilt that's quick and easy to make. Quick-Fuse Appliqué makes these quilts as easy as they are beautiful. Choose from three fun designs for a just-right quilt for a special person.

Finished Size: 24½" x 24½"

Many Thanks Quilt 1 24½" x 24½"	FIRST CUT		SECOND CUT	
	Number of Strips or Pieces	Dimensions	Number of Pieces	Dimensions
Fabric A Background ⅓ yard	1	8½" x 42"	4	8½" squares
Fabric B Sashing ⅛ yard	3	1" x 42"	2 3 2	1" x 18" 1" x 17" 1" x 8½"
Outside Border ⅜ yard	3	3½" x 42"	2 2	3½" x 24" 3½" x 18"
Binding ⅓ yard	3	2¾" x 42"		

Backing - ⅞ yard
Batting - 29" x 29"
Appliqués - Assorted scraps
Lightweight Fusible Web - ½ yard

Fabric and Cutting Requirements

Read all instructions before beginning and use ¼"-wide seam allowances throughout. Read Cutting Strips and Pieces on page 92 prior to cutting fabrics.

Getting Started

This trio of quilts can be made quickly and are perfect for "thank you" gifts or to enhance your décor; make one or all three. Appliqués are added using Quick-Fuse Appliqué and finished with decorative stitching; however, if you use heavyweight fusible web, no stitching is required.

If you prefer hand appliqué, reverse appliqué patterns and add ¼"-wide seam allowance.

Making Quilt 1

This little quilt consists of four appliquéd blocks, each measuring 8½" (unfinished). Each block features a different floral motif.

Assembly

1. Sew one 1" x 8½" Fabric B strip between two 8½" Fabric A squares as shown. Press. Make two.

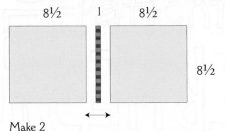

Make 2

2. Arrange and sew together units from step 1 and three 1" x 17" Fabric B strips as shown. Press.

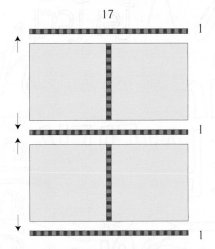

3. Sew unit from step 2 between two 1" x 18" Fabric B strips as shown. Press.

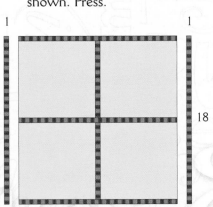

4. Sew 3½" x 18" Outside Border strips to top and bottom of unit from step 3 as shown. Press. Sew 3½" x 24" Outside Border strips to sides. Press. Top measures 24" x 24".

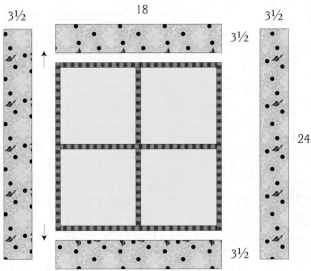

Top measures 24" x 24"

Many Thanks Pattern

Patterns are reversed for use with Quick-Fuse Appliqué (page 93).

Tracing Line ————
Tracing Line --------
(will be hidden behind other fabrics)
Placement Line - - - - -

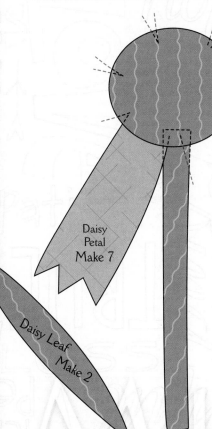

Daisy Petal Make 7

Daisy Leaf Make 2

Adding the Appliqués

1. Refer to Quick-Fuse Appliqué on page 93. Use patterns on pages 76, 77, and below. Trace Quilt 1 Lily, Sunflower, Daisy, and Tulip pieces on fusible web. Use assorted scraps to prepare appliqués for fusing.

2. Refer to photo on page 70 and layout on page 72 to position and fuse flowers to each Fabric A block. Finish appliqués with machine blanket stitch or other decorative stitching as desired.

Layering and Finishing

1. Arrange and baste backing, batting, and top together referring to Layering the Quilt on page 94. Machine or hand quilt as desired.

2. Refer to Binding the Quilt on page 95 and bind quilt to finish.

Milestones

Teamwork

My business began with quilt designs as the foundation. Then painting watercolor artwork for my fabric designs became another piece that seemed to fit right in.

Next, a textile company wanted to print my artwork on kitchen towels and accessories. That was yet another crossroad for me in my career. I was now licensing my art for products in the "home" category. This eventually led to a variety of other home products and dinnerware. At the same time, I started doing stationery and gift products. Today, I have licensing partnerships with over 30 manufacturers.

One of the evolutions that started to happen to me, as new opportunities came along, was being able to bring in more support staff. I now have the benefit of collaboration and a team of wonderful and talented people bringing great ideas to the table.

73

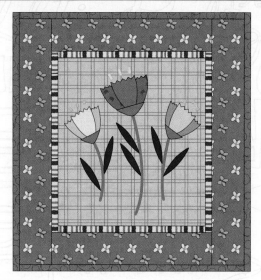

Finished Size: 18½" x 20"

Many Thanks Quilt 2 18½" x 20"	FIRST CUT		SECOND CUT	
	Number of Strips or Pieces	Dimensions	Number of Pieces	Dimensions
Fabric A Background ⅜ yard	1	12" x 13½"		
Accent Border ⅛ yard	2	1" x 42"	2 2	1" x 14½" 1" x 12"
Outside Border ¼ yard	2	3" x 42"	2 2	3" x 19½" 3" x 13"
Binding ¼ yard	2	2¾" x 42"		

Backing - ⅔ yard
Batting - 22" x 24"
Appliqués - Assorted scraps
Assorted Beads
Embroidery Floss
Lightweight Fusible Web - ½ yard

Making Quilt 2

Quilt 2 consists of a center block with three quick-fused flowers in two different sizes. The flowers are embellished with assorted beads, but you can also use embroidery.

Assembly

1. Sew 1" x 12" Accent Border strips to top and bottom of 12" x 13½" Fabric A piece as shown. Press. Sew 1" x 14½" Accent Border strips to sides. Press.

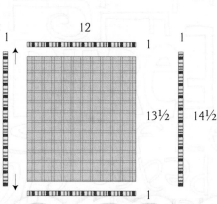

2. Sew 3" x 13" Outside Border strips to top and bottom of unit from step 1 as shown. Press. Sew 3" x 19½" Outside Border strips to sides. Press. Top measures 18" x 19½".

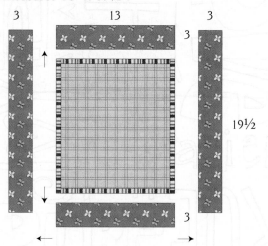

Top measures 18" x 19½"

Adding the Appliqués

1. Refer to Quick-Fuse Appliqué on page 93 and use patterns on pages 76 and 77. Trace Quilt 2 Large Tulip, two Small Tulip pieces, two Stems, and one Stem in reverse onto fusible web. Use assorted scraps to prepare all appliqués for fusing. Refer to layout and photo on page 70 to alter Stem length as needed.

2. Refer to photo on page 70 and layout to position and fuse flowers to quilt center. Finish appliqués with machine satin stitch or other decorative stitching as desired.

Layering and Finishing

1. Arrange and baste backing, batting, and top together referring to Layering the Quilt on page 94. Hand or machine quilt as desired.

2. Refer to Binding the Quilt on page 95 and bind quilt to finish.

3. Refer to photo on page 70 and layout. Sew beads or use embroidery floss to add French knots to embellish tulips, referring to Embroidery Stitch Guide on page 95 as needed.

Finished Size: 15" x 31"

Many Thanks Quilt 3 15" x 31"	FIRST CUT		SECOND CUT	
	Number of Strips or Pieces	Dimensions	Number of Pieces	Dimensions
Fabric A Block 1 Background ⅓ yard	1	8½" x 42"	2	8½" squares
Fabric B Embroidery Background ⅓ yard	1	10" x 7" Trim to 8½" x 5" after embroidering		
Fabric C Block 2 Accent ⅛ yard	1	2¼" x 42"	2	2¼" x 8½"
Accent Border ⅛ yard	2	1" x 42"	2 2	1" x 25½" 1" x 8½"
Outside Border ⅓ yard	3	3" x 42"	2 2	3" x 30½" 3" x 9½"
Binding ⅓ yard	3	2¾" x 42"		

Backing - ⅝ yard
Batting - 19" x 35"
Appliqués - Assorted scraps
Lightweight Fusible Web - ⅓ yard
Embroidery Thread or Floss (optional)
Four Buttons

Making Quilt 3

We used Quick-Fuse Appliqué to create the two 8½" (unfinished) blocks in this quilt. You can highlight the center fabric piece with a machine-embroidered design as we did, with hand embroidery, or use it to showcase a special piece of fabric.

Assembly

1. Type Kindness Matters on a computer using a large, script font to create a template. Using two strands of embroidery floss and a satin stitch, embroider "Kindness Matters" on 10" x 7" Fabric B piece. We used the Bernina® artista 200E and the Cursive Alphabet to embroider the fabric.

2. Use a see-through ruler and rotary cutter to trim embroidered piece to 8½" x 5".

3. Arrange and sew together two 1" x 8½" Accent Border pieces, two 8½" Fabric A squares, two 2¼" x 8½" Fabric C pieces, and 8½" x 5" embroidered piece from step 2 as shown. Press.

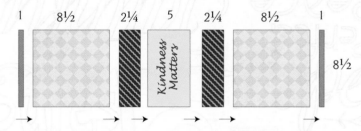

4. Sew unit from step 3 between two 1" x 25½" Accent Border pieces as shown. Press.

5. Sew unit from step 4 between 3" x 9½" Outside Border pieces. Press. Sew this unit between two 3" x 30½" Outside Border pieces. Press.

Adding the Appliqués

1. Refer to Quick-Fuse Appliqué on page 93 and use patterns on page 77 to trace twelve Kindness Flower Petals, two flower centers, and eight leaves on paper side of fusible web. Use assorted scraps to prepare all appliqués for fusing.

2. Refer to photo on page 70 and layout on page 75 to position and fuse appliqués on Fabric A Background blocks. Finish appliqués with machine satin stitch or other decorative stitching as desired.

Layering and Finishing

1. Arrange and baste backing, batting, and top together referring to Layering the Quilt on page 94. Hand or machine quilt as desired.

2. Refer to Binding the Quilt on page 95 and bind quilt to finish.

3. Refer to photo on page 70 and layout on page 75 to position and sew butttons to quilt.

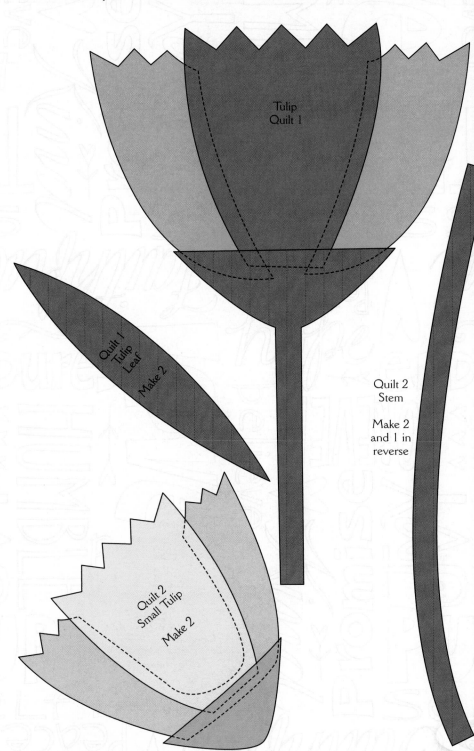

Tulip
Quilt 1

Quilt 1
Tulip
Leaf
Make 2

Quilt 2
Stem

Make 2 and 1 in reverse

Quilt 2
Small Tulip
Make 2

Many Thanks Patterns

Patterns are reversed for use with Quick-Fuse Appliqué (page 93).

Tracing Line ――――――
Tracing Line ‑ ‑ ‑ ‑ ‑ ‑ ‑ ‑
(will be hidden behind other fabrics)

Lily
Quilt 1

Kindness Leaf
Make 8

Kindness
Flower Petal
Quilt 3
Make 12

Lily Leaf
Make 1
and 1
reversed

Kindness
Flower Center
Make 2

Quilt 2
Large Tulip

Sunflower
Quilt 1

Quilt 2
Tulip
Leaf
Make 2

Sunflower Leaf
Make 2

Retirement leads to...

...lifestyle changes, happy challenges, and a fun **change of pace**. Celebrate the **new paths** of retirement with a building block quilt with a diagonal design and a **free-spirited** shape.

A great **retirement gift** from a group, the light-colored sashing provides the perfect place for signatures of **well-wishers**.

As the retiree heads out for **new adventures**-whether it's travel, volunteer activities, gardening, or **hobbies**-this quilt will be a reminder to follow his or her **own path** to later-in-life happiness.

New Paths Quilt

Follow a new path as a quilter with this striking quilt that looks far more complicated than its actual construction. Strip piecing adds ease to block construction and quick corner triangles reduce the need to work with diagonals. Pieces trimmed from the Quick Corner Triangles are reused in the border. This quilt would make a wonderful retirement or going away gift as the light-colored sashing provides perfect places for signatures of well-wishers.

New Paths Quilt 52" x 64¾"	FIRST CUT		SECOND CUT	
	Number of Strips or Pieces	Dimensions	Number of Pieces	Dimensions
Fabric A Light Green Strip ½ yard	7	2" x 42"		
Fabric B Dark Green Strip ⅜ yard	7	1½" x 42"		
Fabric C Medium Green 1⅛ yards	7	5" x 42"		
Fabric D Light Red Strip ½ yard	7	2" x 42"		
Fabric E Dark Red Strip ⅜ yard	7	1½" x 42"		
Fabric F Red Triangle 1⅛ yards	7	5" x 42"		
Fabric G Tan Sashing 1⅓ yards	6	7½" x 42"	38	7½" x 2½"
Fabric H Sashing Squares ⅜ yard	4	2½" x 42"	8	2½" squares
Binding ⅝ yard	6	2¾"" x 42"		
Backing - 3⅙ yards Batting - 57" x 70"				

Fabric and Cutting Requirements

Read all instructions before beginning and use ¼"-wide seam allowances throughout. Read Cutting Strips and Pieces on page 92 prior to cutting fabrics.

Getting Started

Sashing and corner squares make the 7½" (unfinished) blocks in this simple, yet dynamic, quilt appear much larger, while providing space for signatures and other sentiments. Strong diagonal lines, created by an on-point setting, adds visual impact. Our Quick Corner Triangles method makes piecing triangles a snap. We used ten of the leftover triangles to fill in the quilt top; if you wish, you can use the rest to make a smaller version of the same project.

Refer to Accurate Seam Allowance on page 92. Whenever possible, use the Assembly Line Method on page 92. Press seams in direction of arrows.

Making the Blocks

1. Arrange and sew together one 2" x 42" Fabric A strip, one 1½" x 42" Fabric B strip, and one 5" x 42" Fabric C strip as shown to make a strip set. Press. Make seven. Cut thirty-one 7½"-wide segments.

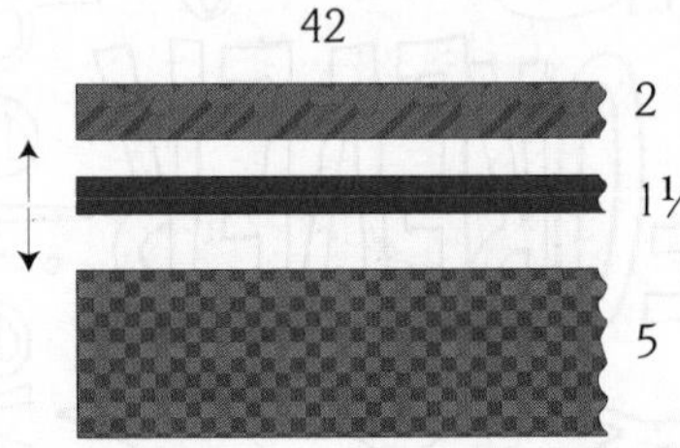

Make 7

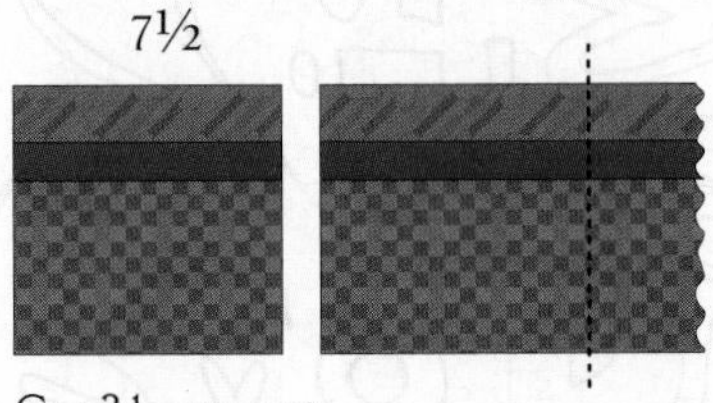

Cut 31 segments

2. Arrange and sew together one 2" x 42" Fabric D strip, one 1½" x 42" Fabric E strip, and one 5" x 42" Fabric F strip as shown to make a strip set. Press. Make seven. Cut thirty-one 7½"-wide segments.

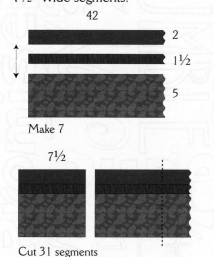

Make 7

Cut 31 segments

3. Refer to Quick Corner Triangles on page 92. Making a quick corner triangle unit, place one unit from step 1 right sides together with one unit from step 2, placing Fabric B perpendicular to Fabric E, Fabric A on the left edge, and Fabric F on the top edge. Fold back the top unit to make sure block looks like diagram, and then sew. Press. Make thirty-one. *Trim carefully ¼" away from stitch line as ten of the trimmed triangles will be used as side-setting triangle corner units.*

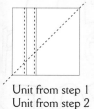

Unit from step 1
Unit from step 2

Make 31

4. Sew one 7½" x 2½" Fabric G piece between two units from step 3.

2½

7½

Make 12

taking care to turn the units as shown. Press. Make twelve.

5. Sew one 7½" x 42" Fabric G strip and one 2½" x 42" Fabric H strip together as shown to make a strip set. Press. Make three. Cut forty-five

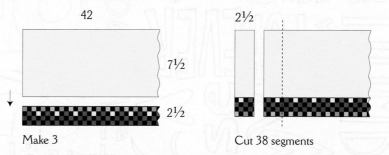

42

7½

2½

Make 3

2½

Cut 38 segments

2½"-wide segments from strip sets.

6. Sew two units from step 5 together as shown. Press. Make eighteen.

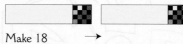

Make 18 →

New Paths Quilt
Finished Size: 52" x 64¾"

81

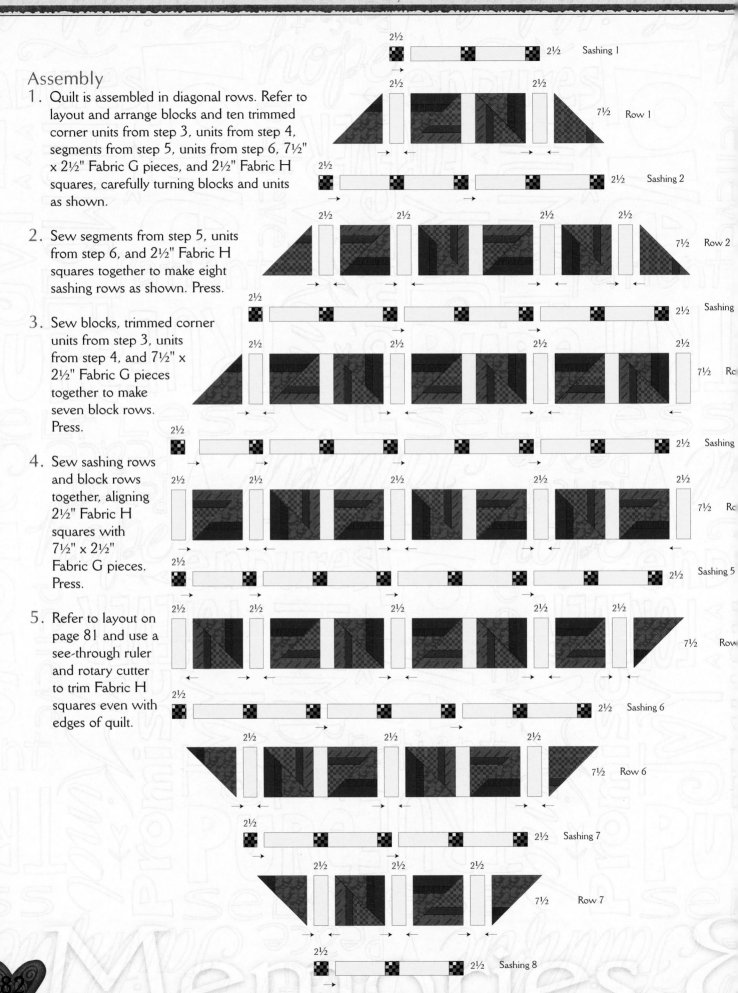

Assembly

1. Quilt is assembled in diagonal rows. Refer to layout and arrange blocks and ten trimmed corner units from step 3, units from step 4, segments from step 5, units from step 6, 7½" x 2½" Fabric G pieces, and 2½" Fabric H squares, carefully turning blocks and units as shown.

2. Sew segments from step 5, units from step 6, and 2½" Fabric H squares together to make eight sashing rows as shown. Press.

3. Sew blocks, trimmed corner units from step 3, units from step 4, and 7½" x 2½" Fabric G pieces together to make seven block rows. Press.

4. Sew sashing rows and block rows together, aligning 2½" Fabric H squares with 7½" x 2½" Fabric G pieces. Press.

5. Refer to layout on page 81 and use a see-through ruler and rotary cutter to trim Fabric H squares even with edges of quilt.

Layering and Finishing

1. Cut backing in half crosswise into two equal pieces. Sew pieces together lengthwise to make one 57" x 80" (approximate) backing piece. Press and trim backing to 57" x 70".

2. Arrange and baste backing, batting, and top together referring to Layering the Quilt on page 94. Machine or hand quilt as desired.

3. Measure diagonal corners of quilt. Add 1" to this measurement and cut four binding strips. Sew to corners of quilt and press.

4. Measure top and bottom widths of quilt including corner bindings. Cut two binding strips to this measurement and sew to top and bottom of quilt. Press.

5. Sew remaining binding strips together end-to-end to make one 2¾"-wide binding strip. Measure side lengths of quilt including corner bindings. Cut two strips to this measurement and sew to sides of quilt. Press.

6. Turn corner bindings to back of quilt first, then side bindings, then top and bottom bindings last. Hand stitch in place.

Milestones

Home away from Home

After a few years, my office/studio moved out of my basement into a small house. Then as staff and stuff grew, we migrated to a small office building. In 1997, we built a specially designed studio to accommodate all of our needs.

Today, we are happily ensconced in our beautiful building. Over the course of a decade, we've added departments, eliminated departments and evolved to a comfortable staff size to focus on our core objective of creating art for products, content for publications and building a lifestyle brand.

Making an Autograph Quilt

An autograph quilt is the perfect keepsake for someone who is retiring, moving away, or following a new path in life. The light-colored sashing in this quilt is ideal for collecting signatures and written sentiments that the recipient will treasure for years to come.

•Have friends sign the sashing strips before they are sewn into the quilt

•Place the sashing strip on a piece of fine sandpaper on a hard surface so it doesn't move around when a friend is signing.

•Use a pen with micro pigment ink for waterproof and fade proof fine lines. We use a Micron®™ pen with archival ink.

•Late-comers can sign on the finished quilt if necessary.

•Be sure to place a label on the back of the quilt giving details of the occasion and the name of the recipient as well as names of the quilt makers.

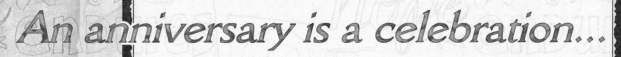

An anniversary is a celebration...

…of the past, and even more,
a **commitment** to the **future**.

It's a chance to recall past
achievements and a time to set
new **goals**. It's an opportunity to
look ahead and plan for a
very **bright future**.

Those achievements and goals
are **represented** in this quilt
with the bold colors and
outreaching motifs
of the four blocks.

Like **spotlights** or
a theater marquee,
this quilt pays tribute
to the past and **announces plans**
for all that is yet to come.

Bright Future Quilt

Like a spotlight or theater marquee, the bold design of this dynamic quilt announces plans for a bright future. Paper-piecing makes construction easy and using striped fabric adds even more delightful detail. Hang this quilt on the wall and get ready for the oohs and ahs!

Bright Future 57" x 57"	FIRST CUT		SECOND CUT	
	Number of Strips or Pieces	Dimensions	Number of Pieces	Dimensions
Fabric A Background Accent & #9 Paper-Pieced Shape 1 yard	2	8½" x 42"	8	8½" squares
	2	7½" x 42"	16	7½" x 4" (#9)
Fabric B Background Accent & #9 Paper Shape 1 yard	2	8½" x 42"	8	8½" squares
	2	7½" x 42"	16	7½" x 4" (#9)
Fabric C Background 2 yards	3	5½" x 42"	16	5½" squares
	2	5" x 42"	16	5" squares
	8	3" x 42"	32	3" x 5" (#1)
			32	3" x 4" (#5)
	4	2½" x 42"	32	2½" x 4½" (#7)
	3	2¼" x 42"	32	2¼" x 3½" (#3)
Fabric D Center & #2 Paper-Pieced Shape ⅝ yard	1	7" x 42"	4	7" squares
	5	2½" x 42"	32	2½" x 5½" (#2)
Fabric E Center Dark Triangles, #4 & #10 Paper-Pieced Shapes 1⅙ yards OR 1¾ yards**	1	7" x 42"	8	7" x 2¼"**
	3	3½" x 42"	32	3½" squares (#10)
	6	2½" x 42"	32	2½" x 6" (#4)
	3	2¼" x 42"	8	2¼" x 10½"**
Fabric F Center Light Triangles & #6 Paper-Pieced Shape ¾ yard	2	4" x 42"	16	4" squares
	6	2½" x 42"	32	2½" x 6½" (#6)
Fabric G #8 Paper-Pieced Shape 1 yard	4	8" x 42"*	32	8" x 4" (#8)
Outside Border ½ yard	6	2½" x 42"		
Binding ⅝ yard	6	2¾" x 42"		

Backing - 3½ yards
Batting - 63" x 63"
*For directional fabric, the size that is listed first runs parallel to selvage (strip width).
**We used diagonally striped fabric, and fussy cut these pieces from four 9" x 42" fabric strips.

Fabric and Cutting Requirements

Read all instructions before beginning and use ¼"-wide seam allowances throughout. Read Cutting Strips and Pieces on page 92 prior to cutting fabrics.

Getting Started

This dazzling, graphic quilt will bring a dramatic touch to any room in your home. It consists of four 26½" square (unfinished) blocks, two each in two different color combinations. Each block is constructed from foundation paper-pieced units and quick corner triangle units.

We used a **diagonally striped fabric** for Fabric E. All pieces were cut on the straight grain with the exception of the 7" x 2¼" and 2¼" x 10" pieces which were cut on the bias. See step 5, page 89, for direction of stripes.

Refer to Accurate Seam Allowance on page 92. Whenever possible, use the Assembly Line Method on page 92. Press seams in the direction of arrows.

Paper-Pieced Units

Copy Bright Future pattern on page 91. If you are using a copier, be sure to compare photocopy to the original pattern to make sure the pattern is accurate (5½" x 8½"). Adjust copier as needed. Make thirty-two copies of pattern: sixteen regular and sixteen reversed. Make all copies from the same copier at the same time to avoid distortions. **Cut paper-piecing copies larger than the trim line on all sides.** Units will be cut on trim line after they are completed. Complete one paper-pieced unit prior to making others to learn technique. Then, use Assembly Line Method on page 92 whenever possible.

1. Center one 3" x 5" Fabric C piece right side up over shape 1 on blank (unprinted) side of Bright Future pattern. Pin to paper using flat flower-head pins. Be sure to cover entire area, extending at least ½" on all sides of shape 1. If it is difficult to see through paper, hold layers up to light to check fabric placement.

2. Turn paper to printed side. Fold paper along stitch line between shapes 1 and 2. Use a card stock or file folder to aid in folding paper as shown.

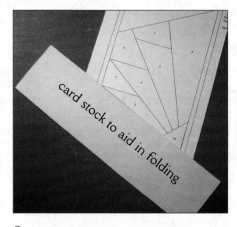

3. Align ¼" mark of ruler with folded edge of paper and trim fabric as shown.

4. Unfold paper. With right sides together, match edges of 2½" x 5½" Fabric D piece with Fabric C piece just trimmed. Pin in place. Turn paper printed-side up and sew on line between shapes 1 and 2 through paper and both layers of fabric using a very short stitch (about 14 to 16 stitches per inch). Begin and end stitches ¼" beyond line. Flip Fabric D piece over to cover seam line. Finger press or lightly press.

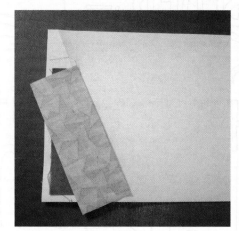
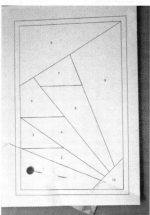

Bright Future Quilt
Finished Size: 57" x 57"

5. Repeat steps 2–4, trimming Fabric D between spaces 2 and 3, and adding 2¼" x 3½" Fabric C piece. Press.

6. Repeat steps 2–4 to add pieces 4 through 10, using 2½" x 6" Fabric E piece (shape 4), 3" x 4" Fabric C piece (shape 5), 2½" x 6½" Fabric F piece (shape 6), 2½" x 4½" Fabric C piece (shape 7), 8" x 4" Fabric G piece (shape 8), 7½" x 4" Fabric A or B piece (shape 9), and 3½" Fabric E square (shape 10). Stay stitch just inside trim line on paper pattern.

7. Repeat steps 1–6 to make thirty-two paper-pieced units: sixteen regular and sixteen reversed, half using Fabric H for Shape 9 and half using Fabric B for Shape 9. This makes eight regular and eight reversed units in each color combination. Units are the same fabric combinations with exception of Shape 9.

8. Trim each block along paper pattern trim line as shown.

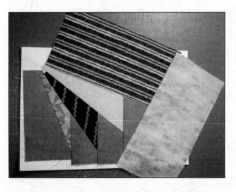
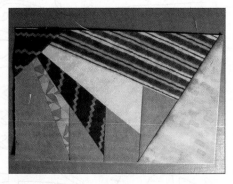

9. Arrange and sew together one regular and one matching reverse paper-pieced unit as shown. Press seam open. Make sixteen, eight of each combination. Remove paper patterns.

Make 16
(8 of each combination)

Blocks

Note: Remember to reset your sewing machine to normal stitch length for remainder of quilt construction.

1. Refer to Quick Corner Triangles on page 92. Making quick corner triangle units, sew one 5" Fabric C square and one 5½" Fabric C square to one 8½" Fabric A square as shown. Press. Make eight.

C = 5 x 5
C = 5½ x 5½
A = 8½ x 8½
Make 8

Make 8

2. Making quick corner triangle units, sew one 5" Fabric C square and one 5½" Fabric C square to one 8½" Fabric B square as shown. Press. Make eight.

C = 5 x 5
C = 5½ x 5½
B = 8½ x 8½
Make 8

Make 8

3. Sew one matching paper-pieced unit between two units from step 1 as shown. Press. Make four.

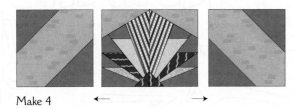

Make 4 ← →

4. Sew one matching paper-pieced unit between two units from step 2 as shown. Press. Make four.

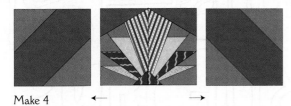

Make 4 ← →

5. Sew one 7" Fabric D square between two 7" x 2¼" Fabric E pieces. Press. Sew this unit between two 2¼" x 10½" Fabric E pieces. Press. Make four.

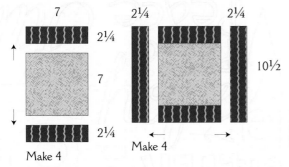

Make 4

Make 4

6. Making quick corner triangle units, sew four 4" Fabric F squares to unit from step 5 as shown. Press. Make four.

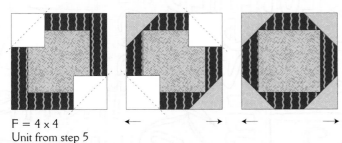

F = 4 x 4
Unit from step 5
Make 4

7. Sew one unit from step 6 between two matching paper-pieced units as shown. Press. Make two.

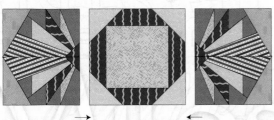

Make 2

Milestones

Upward and Onward

Twenty years have slipped by in the wink of an eye. I've learned and grown, enjoyed successes and worked through challenges, welcomed wonderful people into my life, and, in many ways achieved the humble goals that sent me down this path twenty years ago—Be creative, enjoy my work, and hope to make enough money that I didn't have to get a "real" job!

And, I'm looking forward to the next twenty years with all the fun, creativity, opportunities, and challenges that come with the territory. Thanks for coming along on a great ride!

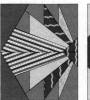

Bead-dazzled Planter

Create a dazzling decorating accessory with paint and beads.

Materials Needed

Tin Flowerpot or Urn
Vinegar
Grey Metal Primer
Acrylic Craft Paints in Medium Green
   and Medium/Dark Green
Sea Sponge and Assorted Paintbrushes
Assorted Large Beads
Gold-Colored 24 Gauge Wire
Drill with small Metal Bit
Matte Spray Varnish
Water-Based Burnt Umber Glaze

Painting the Urn

1. Wash tin urn with vinegar to remove oils and rinse well. When thoroughly dry, spray with metal primer.

2. Basecoat urn with medium green paint and allow to dry.

3. Dampen sea sponge with water and wring thoroughly. Place small amounts of medium green paint and medium/dark green paint on a disposable plate or paper palette. Dip sea sponge in both colors and blot paint by tapping on a paper towel several times. Using a tapping motion, sponge paint onto the urn. Use a light touch to achieve a stippled effect. Refill sponge as necessary, and adjust amount of each color on the sponge to achieve the desired effect. Allow to dry.

4. Spray urn with matte varnish and allow to dry.

5. Apply burnt umber glaze following manufacturer's directions and allow to dry.

6. Spray urn with a final coat of matte varnish.

7. Drill small holes about 1½" apart around rim of urn to feed wire through.

8. Consulting picture and using your own creativity, attach beads and wire to urn, wrapping some beads with wire and adding multiple layers of beads where desired.

8. Sew one unit from step 6 between two matching paper-pieced units as shown. Press. Make two.

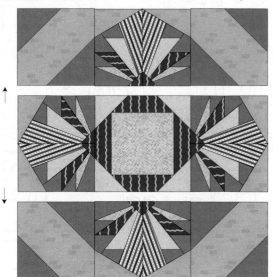

Make 2

9. Sew one unit from step 7 between two units from step 3 as shown. Press. Make two. Block measures 26½" square.

Make 2
Block measures 26½" square

10. Sew one unit from step 8 between two units from step 4 as shown. Press. Make two. Block measures 26½" square.

Make 2
Block measures 26½" square

Assembly

Refer to photo on page 84 and layout on page 87. Arrange and sew blocks in two rows of two blocks each, alternating them as shown. Press seams in opposite directions from row to row. Sew rows together. Press.

Borders

1. Sew 2½" x 42" Fabric E strips together end-to-end to make one continuous 2½"-wide Outside Border strip. Press. Measure quilt through center from side to side. Cut two 2½"-wide Outside Border strips to this measurement. Sew to top and bottom of quilt. Press seams toward border.

2. Measure quilt through center from side to side including borders just added. Cut two 2½"-wide Outside Border strips to this measurement. Sew to sides of quilt. Press.

Layering and Finishing

1. Cut backing in half crosswise into two equal pieces. Sew pieces together lengthwise to make one 63" x 80" (approximate) backing piece. Press and trim to 63" x 63".

2. Arrange and baste backing, batting, and top together, referring to Layering the Quilt on page 94. Hand or machine quilt as desired.

3. Sew 2¾" x 42" binding strips end-to-end to make one continuous 2¾"-wide strip. Refer to Binding the Quilt on page 95 and bind quilt to finish.

Bright Future Foundation Paper-Pieced Pattern
Make 16 and 16 reversed

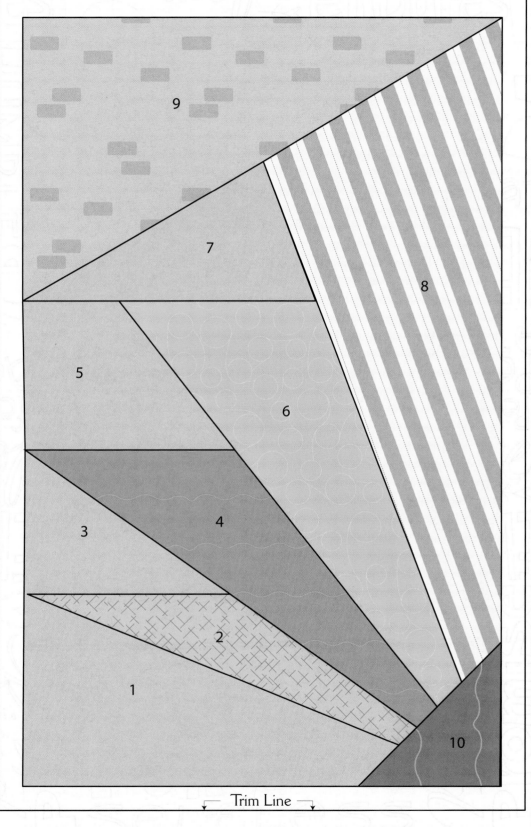

Trim Line

General Directions

Cutting Strips & Pieces

We recommend washing cotton fabrics in cold water and pressing before making projects in this book. Using a rotary cutter, see-through ruler, and a cutting mat, cut the strips and pieces for the project. If indicated on the Cutting Chart, some will need to be cut again into smaller strips and pieces. Make second cuts in order shown to maximize use of fabric. The approximate width of the fabric is 42".

Measurements for all pieces include ¼"-wide seam allowance unless otherwise indicated.

Fussy Cut

To make a "fussy cut," carefully position ruler or template over a selected design in fabric. Include seam allowances before cutting desired pieces.

Assembly Line Method

Whenever possible, use an assembly line method. Position pieces right sides together and line up next to sewing machine. Stitch first unit together, then continue sewing others without breaking threads. When all units are sewn, clip threads to separate. Press seams in the direction of arrows.

Accurate Seam Allowance

Accurate seam allowances are always important, but especially when the blocks contain many pieces and the quilt top contains multiple pieced borders. If each seam is off as little as ¹⁄₁₆", you'll soon find yourself struggling with components that just won't fit.

To ensure seams are a perfect ¼"-wide, try this simple test: Cut three strips of fabric, each exactly 1½" x 12". With right sides together, and long raw edges aligned, sew two strips together, carefully maintaining a ¼" seam. Press seam to one side. Add the third strip to complete the strip set. Press and measure. The finished strip set should measure 3½" x 12". The center strip should measure 1"-wide, the two outside strips 1¼"-wide, and the seam allowances exactly ¼".

If your measurements differ, check to make sure that seams have been pressed flat. If strip set still doesn't "measure up," try stitching a new strip set, adjusting the seam allowance until a perfect ¼"-wide seam is achieved.

Pressing is very important for accurate seam allowances. Press seams using either steam or dry heat with an "up and down" motion. Do not use side-to-side motion as this will distort the unit or block. Set the seam by pressing along the line of stitching, then press seams to one side as indicated by project instructions. Press seams in the direction of arrows.

Quick Corner Triangles

Quick corner triangles are formed by simply sewing fabric squares to other squares or rectangles. The directions and diagrams with each project illustrate what size pieces to use and where to place squares on the corresponding piece. Follow steps 1–3 below to make quick corner triangle units.

1. With pencil and ruler, draw diagonal line on wrong side of fabric square that will form the triangle. This will be your sewing line.

sewing line

2. With right sides together, place square on corresponding piece. Matching raw edges, pin in place, and sew ON drawn line. Trim off excess fabric, leaving ¼"-wide seam allowance as shown.

trim ¼" away
from sewing line

3. Press seam in direction of arrow as shown in step-by-step project diagram. Measure completed quick corner triangle unit to ensure the greatest accuracy.

finished
quick corner
triangle unit

Quick-Fuse Appliqué

Quick-fuse appliqué is a method of adhering appliqué pieces to a background with fusible web. For quick and easy results, simply quick-fuse appliqué pieces in place. Use sewable, lightweight fusible web for the projects in this book unless otherwise indicated. Finishing raw edges with stitching is desirable; laundering is not recommended unless edges are finished.

1. With paper side up, lay fusible web over appliqué pattern. Leaving ½" space between pieces, trace all elements of design. Cut around traced pieces, approximately ¼" outside traced line.

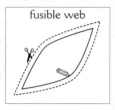
fusible web

2. With paper side up, position and press fusible web to wrong side of selected fabrics. Follow manufacturer's directions for iron temperature and fusing time. Cut out each piece on traced line.

fabric-wrong side

3. Remove paper backing from pieces. A thin film will remain on wrong side of fabric. Position and fuse all pieces of one appliqué design at a time onto background, referring to photos for placement. Fused design will be the reverse of traced pattern.

Appliqué Pressing Sheet

An appliqué pressing sheet is very helpful when there are many small elements to apply using a quick-fuse appliqué technique. The pressing sheet allows small items to be bonded together before applying them to the background. The sheet is coated with a special material that prevents fusible web from adhering permanently to the sheet. Follow manufacturer's directions. Remember to let fabric cool completely before lifting it from the appliqué sheet. If not cooled, the fusible web could remain on the sheet instead of on the fabric.

Machine Appliqué

This technique should be used when you are planning to launder quick-fuse projects. Several different stitches can be used: small narrow zigzag stitch, satin stitch, blanket stitch, or another decorative machine stitch. Use an open toe appliqué foot if your machine has one. Use a stabilizer to obtain even stitches and help prevent puckering. Always practice first to check machine settings.

1. Fuse all pieces following Quick-Fuse Appliqué directions.

2. Cut a piece of stabilizer large enough to extend beyond the area to be stitched. Pin to the wrong side of fabric.

3. Select thread to match appliqué.

4. Following the order that appliqués were positioned, stitch along the edges of each section. Anchor beginning and ending stitches by tying off or stitching in place two or three times.

5. Complete all stitching, then remove stabilizer.

Hand Appliqué

Hand appliqué is easy when you start out with the right supplies. Cotton and machine embroidery thread are easy to work with. Pick a color that matches the appliqué fabric as closely as possible. Use appliqué or silk pins for holding shapes in place and a long, thin needle, such as a sharp, for stitching.

1. Make a template for every shape in the appliqué design. Use a dotted line to show where pieces overlap.

2. Place template on right side of appliqué fabric. Trace around template.

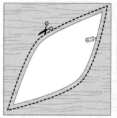

3. Cut out shapes ¼" beyond traced line.

4. Position shapes on background fabric, referring to quilt layout. Pin shapes in place.

5. When layering and stitching appliqué shapes, always work from background to foreground. Where shapes overlap, do not turn under and stitch edges of bottom pieces. Turn and stitch the edges of the piece on top.

6. Use the traced line as your turn-under guide. Entering from the wrong side of the appliqué shape, bring the needle up on the traced line. Using the tip of the needle, turn under the fabric along the traced line. Using blind stitch, stitch along the folded edge to join the appliqué shape to the background fabric. Turn under and stitch about ¼" at a time.

Making Yo-Yos

1. Trace 2½" Yo-Yo Template on wrong side of fabric and cut out on drawn Line.

2. Hold the circle with the wrong side facing you. Fold edge toward you turning ¼" and use quilting thread to sew short running stitches close to folded edge.

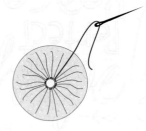

Wrong side

3. Pull thread tightly to gather into a smaller circle. Make several invisible "tacking" stitches to secure the thread.

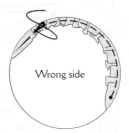

4. Refer to color photo and quilt layout to position and tack yo-yos in place.

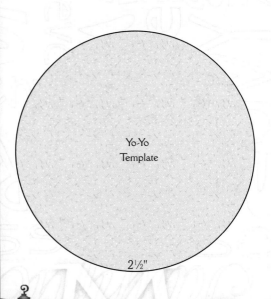

Yo-Yo Template

2½"

Adding the Borders

1. Measure quilt through the center from side to side. Trim two border strips to this measurement. Sew to top and bottom of quilt. Press seams toward border.

2. Measure quilt through the center from top to bottom, including borders added in step 1. Trim border strips to this measurement. Sew to sides and press. Repeat to add additional borders.

Mitered Borders

A mitered border is usually "fussy cut" to highlight a motif or design. Borders are cut slightly longer than needed to allow for centering of motif or matching corners.

1. Cut the border strips or strip sets as indicated for quilt.

2. Measure each side of the quilt and mark center with a pin. Fold each border strip in half crosswise to find its midpoint and mark with a pin. Using the side measurements, measure out from the midpoint and place a pin to show where the edges of the quilt will be.

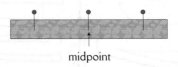

midpoint

3. Align a border strip to quilt. Pin at midpoints and pin-marked ends first, then along entire side, easing to fit if necessary.

4. Sew border to quilt, stopping and starting ¼" from pin-marked end points. Repeat to sew all four border strips to quilt.

quilt front

5. Fold corner of quilt diagonally, right sides together, matching seams and borders. Place a long ruler along fold line extending across border. Draw a diagonal line across border from fold to edge of border. This is the stitching line. Starting at ¼" mark, stitch on drawn line. Check for squareness, then trim excess. Press seam open.

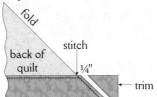

fold

stitch

back of quilt

¼"

trim

Layering the Quilt

1. Cut backing and batting 4" to 8" larger than quilt top.

2. Lay pressed backing on bottom (right side down), batting in middle, and pressed quilt top (right side up) on top. Make sure everything is centered and that backing and batting are flat. Backing and batting will extend beyond quilt top.

3. Begin basting in center and work toward outside edges. Baste vertically and horizontally, forming a 3"–4" grid. Baste or pin completely around edge of quilt top. Quilt as desired. Remove basting.

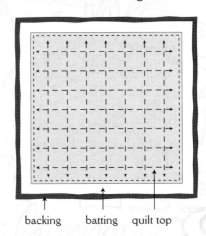

backing   batting   quilt top

Binding the Quilt

1. Trim batting and backing to ¼" beyond raw edge of quilt top. This will add fullness to binding.

2. Join binding strips to make one continuous strip if needed. To join, place strips perpendicular to each other, right sides together, matching diagonal cut edges and allowing tips of angles to extend approximately ¼" beyond edges. Sew ¼"-wide seams. Continue stitching ends together to make the desired length. Press seams open.

3. Fold and press binding strips in half lengthwise with wrong sides together.

4. Measure quilt through center from side to side. Cut two binding strips to this measurement. Lay binding strips on top and bottom edges of quilt top with raw edges of binding and quilt top aligned. Sew through all layers, ¼" from quilt edge. Press binding away from quilt top.

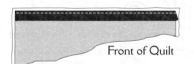
Front of Quilt

5. Measure quilt through center from top to bottom, including binding just added. Cut two binding strips to this measurement and sew to sides through all layers, including binding just added. Press.

6. Folding top and bottom first, fold binding around to back then repeat with sides. Press and pin in position. Hand-stitch binding in place using a blind stitch.

← fold top and bottom binding in first

Finishing Pillows

1. Layer batting between pillow top and lining. Baste. Hand or machine quilt as desired, unless otherwise indicated. Trim batting and lining even with raw edge of pillow top.

2. Narrow hem one long edge of each backing piece by folding under ¼" to wrong side. Press. Fold under ¼" again to wrong side. Press. Stitch along folded edge.

3. With right sides up, lay one backing piece over second piece so hemmed edges overlap, making backing unit the same measurement as the pillow top. Baste backing pieces together at top and bottom where they overlap.

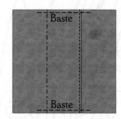

4. With right sides together, position and pin pillow top to backing. Using ¼"-wide seam, sew around edges, trim corners, turn right side out, and press.

Pillow Forms

Cut two pieces of fabric to finished size of pillow form plus ½". Place right sides together, aligning raw edges. Using ¼"-wide seam, sew around all edges, leaving 4" opening for turning. Trim corners and turn right side out. Stuff to desired fullness with polyester fiberfill and hand-stitch opening closed.

Embroidery Stitch Guide

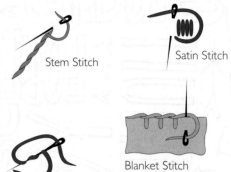
Stem Stitch   Satin Stitch

French Knot

Blanket Stitch

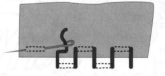
Running Stitch

Blind Stitch

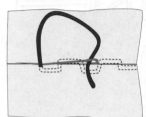
Primitive Stitch

Couching Technique

Couching is a method of attaching a textured yarn, cord, or fiber to fabric for decorative purposes. Use an open-toe embroidery foot, couching foot, or a zigzag presser foot and matching or monofilament thread. Sew with a long zigzag stitch just barely wider than the cord or yarn. Stabilizer on the wrong side of fabric is recommended. Place the yarn, cord, or fiber on right side of fabric and zigzag to attach as shown. A hand-stitch can be used if desired.

Couching

About Debbie Mumm

For twenty years, Debbie Mumm's charming designs and distinctive style have captured the hearts and imaginations of quilters everywhere.

A talented designer and entrepreneur, Debbie got her start in the quilting industry in 1986 with her unique and simple-to-construct quilt patterns. From this beginning, Debbie has led her company to become a multi-faceted enterprise that includes publishing, fabric design, and licensed art divisions.

The author of more than fifty books, Debbie shares her distinctive style with consumers by providing easy-to-follow instructions for quilt and craft projects as well as home decorating tips and inspiration.

At the heart of Debbie's design you will find the warmth and richness of country tradition. Her creative passion is to bring that feeling and those traditional elements together with fresh palettes and modern themes to create the look of today's modern country.

Debbie Mumm celebrates **20** years of Creativity 1986~2006

Designs by Debbie Mumm®

Special thanks to my creative teams:

Editorial & Project Design

Carolyn Ogden: Managing Editor • Georgie Gerl: Quilt Designer • Carolyn Lowe: Quilt Designer
Jean Van Bockel: Quilt Designer • Nancy Kirkland: Seamstress/Quilter/Quilt Designer
Darra Williamson: Technical Editor • Jackie Saling: Craft Designer • Kris Clifford: Papercraft Designer
Pam Clarke: Machine Quilter

Book Design & Production

Tom Harlow: Graphics Manager • Heather Hughes: Graphic Designer
Heather Butler: Graphic Designer • Kathy Rickel: Art Studio Assistant

Photography

Peter Hassel Photography • Debbie Mumm® Graphics Studio

Art Team

Kathy Arbuckle: Artist/Designer • Heather Butler: Artist

The Debbie Mumm® Sewing Studio exclusively uses Bernina® sewing machines.
©2006 Debbie Mumm

Published by:
Leisure Arts, Inc.
5701 Ranch Drive
Little Rock, AR 72223

The information in this publication is presented in good faith, but no warranty is given, nor results guaranteed. Since we have no control over physical conditions surrounding the application of information herein contained, Leisure Arts, Inc. and Debbie Mumm, Inc. disclaim any liability for untoward results.

Produced by:
Debbie Mumm, Inc.
1116 E. Westview Court
Spokane, WA 99218
(509) 466-3572
Fax (509) 466-6919

www.debbiemumm.com